D1715456

HISTORY OF CRIME AND PUNISHMENT

CAPITAL PUNISHMENT

BY DUCHESS HARRIS, JD, PHD
WITH VALERIE BODDEN

Essential Library
An Imprint of Abdo Publishing | abdobooks.com

ABDOBOOKS.COM

Published by Abdo Publishing, a division of ABDO, PO Box 398166, Minneapolis, Minnesota 55439. Copyright © 2020 by Abdo Consulting Group, Inc. International copyrights reserved in all countries. No part of this book may be reproduced in any form without written permission from the publisher. Essential Library™ is a trademark and logo of Abdo Publishing.

Printed in the United States of America, North Mankato, Minnesota.
042019
092019

Interior Photos: Kiichiro Sato/AP Images, 5, 63; Texas Department of Criminal Justice/AP Images, 7; CJ Hanevy/Shutterstock Images, 10; Jay Janner/Statesman.com/Austin American-Statesman/AP Images, 13; Virginia Department of Corrections/AP Images, 17; Shutterstock Images, 19; North Wind Picture Archives, 20; Gabrielle Hilk/The Wilmington News-Journal/AP Images, 21; Aleksandr Stezhkin/Shutterstock Images, 24; Image Source/iStockphoto, 31, 37; Red Line Editorial, 34–35; Amber Hunt/AP Images, 42–43; Steve Ruark/AP Images, 44; Mark Foley/AP Images, 49; Eric Risberg/AP Images, 53; Mark Boster/Los Angeles Times/Getty Images, 55; Bettmann/Getty Images, 57; Bita Honarvar/Atlanta Journal-Constitution/AP Images, 60; Jack Smith/AP Images, 67; Katarzyna Bialasiewicz/iStockphoto, 71; Toby Talbot/AP Images, 73; Tom Dodge/Columbus Dispatch/AP Images, 79; Marvin Fong/The Plain Dealer/AP Images, 80; Alexander Raths/Shutterstock Images, 84; Spencer Platt/Getty Images News/Getty Images, 89; Rich Pedroncelli/AP Images, 92; Alex Wong/Getty Images News/Getty Images, 95

Editor: Charly Haley
Series Designer: Dan Peluso

LIBRARY OF CONGRESS CONTROL NUMBER: 2018966054

PUBLISHER'S CATALOGING-IN-PUBLICATION DATA

Names: Harris, Duchess, author | Bodden, Valerie, author.
Title: Capital punishment / by Duchess Harris and Valerie Bodden
Description: Minneapolis, Minnesota: Abdo Publishing, 2020 | Series: History of crime and punishment | Includes online resources and index.
Identifiers: ISBN 9781532119170 (lib. bdg.) | ISBN 9781532173356 (ebook)
Subjects: LCSH: Capital punishment--Juvenile literature. | Death penalty--Juvenile literature. | Capital punishment--History--Juvenile literature. | Capital punishment--United States--History--Juvenile literature.
Classification: DDC 345.730773--dc23

CONTENTS

CHAPTER ONE

LIFE AND DEATH

A window shows a view of the death chamber at the Southern Ohio Corrections Facility in Lucasville, where inmates sentenced to the death penalty are killed by lethal injection.

On July 14, 1995, a Houston, Texas, television station received a strange call. The caller told the station where to find the body of 16-year-old Dana Sanchez. Sanchez had disappeared a week earlier while hitchhiking to her boyfriend's house. Before he hung up, the caller also gave the station a chilling message. He said that a serial killer was on the loose.

Houston police had already begun to fear this was the case. Sanchez was the fourth young Hispanic woman killed in the same distinctive way since 1986. In all four cases, the killer had strangled his victims to death with a homemade tourniquet of nylon cord tightened with items such as a stick or a toothbrush. His method of killing earned him the nickname the Tourniquet Killer.

Police had a hunch that the person who had called the television station was the killer. For years, they tried to track him down. By 2003, the case had gone cold. But that year, police were able to match a small sample of DNA from under the fingernail of the killer's second victim, 21-year-old Maria del Carmen Estrada. The DNA identified the killer as 41-year-old Anthony Shore, who had been arrested in 1998 for molesting his daughters. Although he'd had to provide a DNA sample upon his arrest, problems at the Houston

Police Department's crime lab led to a five-year delay in the processing of that DNA.

Once the match was identified, however, police were quick to arrest Shore. He soon confessed to the homicide. He also confessed to killing three other young girls, including Sanchez. A jury found Shore guilty and sentenced him to death.

On January 18, 2018, guards led Shore into the execution chamber at the Texas State Penitentiary in Huntsville. As he

Anthony Shore, known as the Tourniquet Killer, was executed by capital punishment in 2018.

THE MOST NOTORIOUS EXECUTIONS

More than 1,400 people have been executed in the United States since 1976.[5] The most notorious among them include:

- Ted Bundy: Between 1974 and 1978, infamous serial killer Bundy killed at least 30 people. He was executed by electrocution in 1989.
- John Wayne Gacy: A serial killer, Gacy spent his free time working as a clown at children's events. Between 1972 and 1978, he killed 33 young men in Cook County, Illinois. He died by lethal injection in 1994.
- Timothy McVeigh: In 1995, McVeigh bombed the Alfred P. Murrah Federal Building in Oklahoma City, Oklahoma, killing 168 people. When he was executed by lethal injection in 2001, he claimed victory over the US government, citing the score as 168–1.
- Aileen Wuornos: One of the few women sentenced to death in US history, Wuornos killed seven men, whom she said had tried to rape her. She was executed by lethal injection in 2002.
- Stanley Williams: The leader of a Los Angeles, California, gang, Williams received a death sentence for the murder of at least four people. While on death row, Williams wrote several books aimed at ending gang violence. He was executed by lethal injection in 2005.

was strapped to the gurney, Shore spoke his final words. Voice cracking, he said, "No amount of words or apology could ever undo what I've done. I wish I could undo the past, but it is what it is."[1] Then, as the technician injected the powerful sedative pentobarbital into his veins, Shore said, "Oooh-ee! I can feel that."[2] Thirteen minutes later, he was dead.

Few people mourned his passing. "Fair is fair, and right is right," Shore's father, Rob Shore, said.[3] Shore's daughter, 32-year-old Tiffany Hall, said her father's death would bring relief that "he can't inflict any kind of damage on anybody else ever again."[4]

"Anthony Allen Shore's reign of terror is officially over," Andy Kahan, who worked for the city of Houston helping crime victims, announced after Shore's death. "There's a reason we have the death penalty in the state of Texas and Anthony Shore is on the top of the list."[6]

TOO YOUNG TO DIE

On September 9, 1993, in Fenton, Missouri, 17-year-old Christopher Simmons and 15-year-old Charlie Benjamin discussed how cool it would be to kill someone. Later that night, they decided to find out for themselves. They chose a random house and broke into it. Inside, they found 46-year-old Shirley Crook. They tied her up and took her to a bridge. There, they threw her, still bound, into the river below, where she drowned.

Simmons and Benjamin, who bragged to friends about what they'd done, were arrested and tried for murder. Because he was only 15, Benjamin could not be sentenced to death. Instead, he was sentenced to life in prison. Simmons, however, received a death sentence. But after he had spent nearly ten years on death row, Simmons's case came before the Missouri Supreme Court. The court commuted, or reduced, his sentence to life in prison, saying he had been

Shirley Crook drowned after she was thrown off a bridge like this one. Most murders are not drownings, however. Most are the result of gunfire.

too young to be sentenced to death. In 2005, Simmons's case came before the US Supreme Court, which had previously set the minimum age for the death penalty at 16. The Supreme Court heard evidence from scientists and psychologists who said the adolescent brain was not fully developed. Thus, the experts contended, those younger than 18 could not be held as culpable for their actions as adults could be. In its 5–4 decision, the court declared capital punishment unconstitutional for anyone who was younger than 18 at the time he or she committed the crime. Simmons's new sentence of life in prison would stand.

KILLING THE INNOCENT

On December 23, 1991, flames roared from the Corsicana, Texas, home where Cameron Todd Willingham lived with his wife and three young daughters. By the time emergency services arrived on the scene, Willingham was running back and forth in front of the house, screaming that his babies were inside. He tried more than once to get back into the house. But it was too late. All three girls died.

In the days after the fire, an arson investigator worked to determine how the fire had started. After examining the structure, the investigator said it was a clear-cut case of arson. He pointed out areas where he said staining indicated that an accelerant, such as gasoline, had been poured on the floors. He said the fire had started in three separate places, a clear indication of arson. Since Willingham had been the only one home with the girls, he was the obvious suspect. He was arrested, tried in court, and sentenced to death.

LAST MEALS

In some states, death row prisoners are allowed to choose their last meal before their execution. Over the years, prisoners have chosen everything from an elaborate lobster dinner to a single olive. If a prisoner can't decide what to eat, he might be served a traditional meal of steak, eggs, hash browns, and toast. Some states set limits on how much a prisoner's last meal can cost. The limit is $40 in Florida and $15 in Oklahoma.[7] In recent years, some states have abolished the practice of last meals. Those being readied for execution eat whatever the other prisoners are being served that day.

COMMUTING THE DEATH PENALTY FOR EVERYONE

When George Ryan became governor of Illinois in 1999, he supported the death penalty. But investigations by students at Northwestern University in Chicago uncovered more than a dozen Illinois cases in which death sentences were secured by faulty eyewitness testimony and forced confessions. The investigations led Ryan to conclude that the criminal justice system in his state was flawed. In 2003, only days before leaving office, Ryan commuted the sentences of all 167 death row inmates to life in prison. "The legislature couldn't reform it. Lawmakers won't repeal it. But I will not stand for it," Ryan said. "I must act."[4] In 2011, Illinois outlawed the use of capital punishment.

After more than a decade on death row, Willingham was put in contact with renowned arson inspector Gerald Hurst. After viewing videos, photos, and the testimony of the original fire inspectors, Hurst concluded those original investigators had based their conclusions on outdated theories about fire. The fire hadn't been a result of arson, Hurst said. Rather, it was likely from a space heater in the children's bedroom. Tests for an accelerant came back positive in only one location: near the front door, where the family stored lighter fluid for their grill. The staining in other spots was the result of the fire's intensity, Hurst reported. He found no indication that the fire had started in more than one location. The evidence was taken to the Texas Board of Pardons and Paroles with an application for clemency. Only four days before his scheduled execution, Willingham learned the board's decision: his application for clemency was denied. On February 17, 2004, Willingham was executed by lethal injection. In his last words, he said he was "an innocent man convicted of a crime I did not commit."[9] At least nine fire investigators who have examined the case since Willingham's death have concluded that the fire that killed his daughters was not a result of arson.[10]

CAPITAL CONTROVERSY

Capital punishment, also referred to as the death penalty, is the execution of a convicted criminal by the government. Considered the ultimate punishment, the death penalty has

After the execution of Cameron Todd Willingham, several advocates have highlighted his case as an example of wrongful execution and a reason to abolish the death penalty.

DEATH FOR THE BOSTON MARATHON BOMBER?

In 2015, the trial of Dzhokhar Tsarnaev ignited fresh debate over the death penalty. In 2013, Tsarnaev and his brother set off bombs at the Boston Marathon, killing three people and injuring 260. Some survivors, including Adrianne Haslet-Davis, who lost a leg in the attack, supported sentencing Tsarnaev to death. She hoped it would serve as a warning that "when you take lives, yours can be taken as well."[12] Other survivors, including Bill and Denise Richard, whose eight-year-old son was killed in the attack, spoke out against the death penalty. They said the lengthy death penalty process would condemn them to years of "reliving the most painful day of our lives."[13] On May 15, 2015, Tsarnaev was sentenced to death.

been used throughout history, from the cross of ancient Rome to the lethal injection employed in the United States today. Although many countries now prohibit capital punishment, 30 US states and the US federal government continue to sentence criminals to death.[11]

The cases of Anthony Shore, Christopher Simmons, and Cameron Todd Willingham illustrate some of the many complex and controversial issues surrounding the death penalty. Do those who kill others deserve to die themselves? Should some people be put to death but not others who commit the same kinds of crimes? What if an innocent person is executed?

Supporters and opponents of the death penalty raise both moral and practical arguments as they debate its use. Supporters say the death penalty is what the worst criminals deserve. But opponents argue that killing another person is always wrong, even when that killing is carried out by the state. Supporters also argue that the threat of death stops at least some people from committing violent crimes. Opponents contend that the death penalty is administered unfairly. The two sides debate the costs of the death penalty and its alternatives as well.

Today, capital punishment cases come before the US Supreme Court on a regular basis. So far, the court has maintained that the death penalty is constitutional. But those working to abolish the death penalty believe it is only a matter of time before the court changes this stance. No matter what the Supreme Court ultimately decides, the issue of whether the government has the right to put people to death will likely remain hotly contested for years to come.

DISCUSSION STARTERS

- Why do you think a death row inmate might apologize before his or her execution? How do you think the families of victims might feel about that apology?
- Do you agree with the Supreme Court that people younger than 18 are too young to be held fully responsible for their crimes?
- What should the government do if it learns an innocent person has been executed?

CHAPTER TWO

THE HISTORY OF EXECUTION

Electric chairs were used for executions primarily in the 1890s and early 1900s.

As long as crime has been a feature of society, so has punishment. The history of capital punishment dates back to ancient times. The ancient Greeks instituted capital punishment in cases of murder, treason, arson, and rape. The ancient Romans continued this practice, often adopting particularly painful methods, including crucifixion and drowning in a sealed bag. Capital punishment continued to be applied in Europe throughout the Middle Ages. Those convicted of a crime could be hanged or beheaded. Sometimes, in rare cases, convicted criminals were boiled in oil or drawn and quartered, which is a method of execution that involves tying a person's limbs to animals and then driving the animals In different directions. After the guillotine was invented in the late 1700s, it became a common method of capital punishment.

THE EARLY AMERICAN DEATH PENALTY

When the first British colonists came to North America in the 1600s, they brought with them the practice of capital punishment. Because there were initially no prisons in the colonies, people who committed crimes faced banishment, fines, corporal punishment, or death. Among the crimes that could result in a death sentence were murder, treason,

The last known capital punishment execution carried out by guillotine was in France in 1977. France has since abolished capital punishment.

robbery, rape, and arson. In some colonies, lesser crimes,

such as horse theft and witchcraft, could lead to a death

sentence as well.

Criminal justice was typically quick in colonial America.

After being sentenced to death, a person was given a few

weeks to get his or her affairs in order. The person was also

visited by ministers, who intended to lead the person to

repent of his or her crimes before death. Because part of the

A man convicted of witchcraft, a crime in colonial times, prepares to be hanged publicly in the late 1600s.

purpose of capital punishment was to deter other potential criminals from committing similar crimes, early American executions were carried out publicly. Although they were supposed to be solemn events, the crowds of up to 50,000 that gathered often became rowdy.

Hanging quickly became the main method of execution used in colonial America. It generally led to a quick death. But miscalculations of the rope length or how far the prisoner should drop sometimes led to slow, painful deaths or, at the other extreme, to decapitations. After a hanging, the body was often left on display to serve as a warning to other would-be criminals.

THE ABOLITION MOVEMENT

By the late 1700s, Enlightenment thinkers in Italy, France, England, and America began to speak out against capital punishment. In 1764, Italian economist Cesare Beccaria wrote of the death penalty, "It seems to me absurd that the laws, which are an expression of public will, which detest and punish homicide, should themselves commit it, and that to deter citizens from murder they order a public one."[1] Beccaria's writings influenced several American leaders. Over time, some states began to set limits on the crimes to which capital punishment could be applied. But in many places,

A movement to abolish the death penalty in the United States still exists today.

21

capital punishment remained a mandatory sentence for certain crimes, including murder.

By the 1800s, a full-scale movement to abolish, or end, the death penalty had taken shape. Groups such as the American Society for the Abolition of Capital Punishment lobbied against the death penalty. By the mid-1800s, death sentences in some states were no longer carried out publicly. In 1846, Michigan became the first US territory to ban the death penalty except in cases of treason. Soon afterward, Wisconsin and Rhode Island ended capital punishment for all crimes. Over time, other states followed suit.

NEW METHODS

Even as the debate raged over death sentences, a new method of carrying them out was invented: electrocution. For this method of execution, the convicted prisoner was strapped into a wooden chair, which came to be known as the electric chair. Wet sponges connected to wires were placed on the inmate's head and back. Then the electricity was turned on. The first electrocution, carried out in 1890, included two separate electric shocks. The process took more than eight minutes. The condemned man's body smoldered and caught fire before he died. Even so, electrocution was

THE INVENTION OF THE ELECTRIC CHAIR

The electric chair developed out of fierce competition between inventors Thomas Edison and George Westinghouse in the late 1800s during the early days of electricity. Edison's electrical company employed a direct current (DC) to distribute electricity to much of Manhattan, New York. But Westinghouse proposed that alternating current (AC) electricity would be easier to distribute across a wide geographical area. In his attempts to promote DC electricity, Edison set out to prove that AC electricity was dangerous. He hosted public demonstrations using AC electricity to electrocute animals.

Some saw the potential to use electricity for human executions as well. But both Edison and Westinghouse recognized that the use of their electric generators for executions would bring them bad publicity. Both tried to convince the government to use their competitor's product. Edison was successful. In 1890, the first man was executed using AC electricity. The press soon reported that the man had been "Westinghoused."[3] Over time, however, this method of execution came to be known simply as the electric chair.

quickly hailed as a more humane method of execution than hanging or a firing squad.

But some people continued to feel uneasy about electrocution. In 1921, Nevada introduced the gas chamber. Ten other states eventually followed suit, though few used it for long.[2] In most states, the gas chamber was a small, airtight room with a chair. The executioner flipped a lever that released cyanide pellets into acid, creating a toxic gas. The prisoner died from inhaling the gas, usually after about 15 minutes.

THE SUPREME COURT STEPS IN

Throughout the 1930s and 1940s, record numbers of prisoners were executed. But by the 1950s and 1960s, public

The US Supreme Court building in Washington, DC

opinion had swung against the death penalty. In 1972, the US Supreme Court reviewed three death penalty cases, today known collectively as *Furman v. Georgia*. Lawyers for the defendants argued that the death penalty violated both the Eighth and Fourteenth Amendments to the US Constitution. The Eighth Amendment protects those convicted of crimes from cruel and unusual punishment. The Fourteenth Amendment ensures people equal protection under the law, meaning that all people, regardless of race, must have equal access to legal resources. As they considered the *Furman* case, the Supreme Court justices took into account a concept they had defined in an earlier, unrelated case: evolving standards of decency. This concept holds that a punishment that may have been acceptable when the Constitution was written in 1787 may no longer be acceptable under current standards because society is always evolving.

The justices voted 5–4 that although capital punishment itself wasn't unconstitutional, the way it was imposed at that time violated the Constitution. Justice Potter Stewart wrote:

> These death sentences are cruel and unusual in the same way that being struck by lightning is cruel and unusual. . . . Petitioners are among a capriciously selected random handful upon whom the sentence of death has in fact been imposed. . . . The Eighth and Fourteenth Amendments cannot tolerate the infliction of a sentence of death under legal systems that permit this unique penalty to be so wantonly and so freakishly imposed.[4]

As a result of the court's ruling, a moratorium, or legal stop, was put on all death sentences. The more than 600 inmates on death row had their sentences commuted to life in prison.[5]

Four years later, however, the Supreme Court heard a new death penalty case, *Gregg v. Georgia*. Since the *Furman* decision hadn't declared the death penalty itself unconstitutional, the state of Georgia had rewritten its death penalty statutes. The new statutes specified that the death penalty could only be applied to cases of murder, established

a separate sentencing trial in capital cases, and required the

consideration of aggravating and mitigating factors during

sentencing. In a 7–2 decision, the Supreme Court ruled that

Georgia's new provisions ensured that the death penalty

was applied equally and thus was constitutional. After

the *Gregg* ruling, other states also began to reinstate their

death penalties.

THE DEATH PENALTY TODAY

With the death penalty reinstated, states turned to yet

another new method of execution: lethal injection. First used

in Texas in 1982, lethal injection is

the primary method of execution

today. Initially, most lethal

injections were carried out using

a combination of three drugs.

These drugs included a sedative,

which makes people sleep; a drug

to paralyze the muscles, including

the diaphragm, which is needed

for breathing; and potassium

chloride, a drug that stops the

WHY THREE DRUGS?

The three-drug formula for lethal injection was developed by Oklahoma medical examiner Jay Chapman in 1977. Initially, the formula called for the use of two drugs, which Chapman explained was "to make sure if one didn't kill [the prisoner], the other would." When asked why a third drug was later added, Chapman explained, "You just wanted to make sure the prisoner was dead at the end, so why not just add a third lethal drug?"[6]

heart. The entire process took less than ten minutes. Death penalty advocates touted lethal injection as the most humane method of execution yet.

Throughout the late 1970s and into the 1980s, the number of executions rose. By the 1990s, with crime levels soaring, death sentences had reached their highest level since the *Furman* decision. But by the early 2000s, the trend had reversed, and the number of death sentences handed out began to fall sharply.

BACKUP METHODS

Lethal injection is the primary method of execution in the United States today. In some states, it is the only method of execution allowed. However, a handful of states still allow backup methods in case lethal injection is ever ruled unconstitutional. Utah retains death by firing squad as a backup method. New Hampshire and Washington allow for the use of hanging. The gas chamber and the electric chair also remain legal in some states. Prisoners in some states have the option to choose these alternate methods of execution in place of lethal injection.

Throughout the 2000s, the death penalty has continued to face challenges in court. In 2002, the Supreme Court ruled that the execution of people who are intellectually disabled is unconstitutional. In 2005, the court made the same determination for executions of people who were younger than 18 at the time they committed their crimes.

By 2009, many states found it difficult to obtain the drugs they needed to carry out executions. European drug manufacturers, which are the primary sources of these drugs, refused to sell drugs for use in executions. As a result, some states switched to a single sedative drug for lethal injection.

As of May 2018, Alabama, Mississippi, and Oklahoma had approved a new method of execution: nitrogen hypoxia. This execution method involves the inhalation of nitrogen gas, an odorless substance that quickly replaces oxygen in the body, leading to death. In August 2018, Nebraska became the first state to use the powerful opioid fentanyl for an execution. At that time, Nevada state officials were also looking into using fentanyl for executions.

CHINESE DEATH VANS

As of 2011, 55 crimes were punishable by death in China.[9] In many cases, special death vans travel to Chinese cities and villages. Condemned prisoners are taken into the back of the vans, where lethal injection is administered. The vans are supposed to save money on building execution chambers. They also ensure that those convicted of crimes are executed close to where they committed their offense. Officials say this helps deter others from committing the same crimes. After the execution, doctors in the van harvest the organs to be used for transplants.

THE DEATH PENALTY AROUND THE WORLD

Beginning in the 1970s, many countries around the world abolished the death penalty. As of 2018, about 53 of the world's 195 countries retained the death penalty.[7] Other countries still technically allowed capital punishment but had not executed anyone in a decade or more. In 2017, the

United States was ranked eighth in number of executions worldwide, with 23 people put to death that year.[8]

Of the countries that continue to implement the death penalty, China executes the most people every year. Although official numbers are kept secret by the Chinese government, Amnesty International, a human rights organization, believes that China carries out thousands of executions each year. Iran, Saudi Arabia, and Iraq each execute hundreds of people a year. In many of these countries, people are executed for minor offenses, often publicly and without a formal trial. Forms of execution used around the world include lethal injection, hanging, beheading, and stoning.

DISCUSSION STARTERS

- What might life in the United States be like today if prisons had never been built? Do you think there would be more crime or less?
- Do you agree that lethal injection is the most humane method of execution?
- Why do you think some countries execute hundreds of people every year while others execute none?

CHAPTER THREE

HOW CAPITAL PUNISHMENT WORKS

Prosecuting a death penalty charge and appealing a death
sentence are both lengthy court processes.

As of 2018, 30 states allowed the death penalty, as did the federal government and the US military. Twenty states and Washington, DC, had outlawed capital punishment.[1] Between 1976, when the death penalty was reinstated, and 2018, more than 1,490 people were executed nationwide. Six states accounted for nearly 70 percent of executions in that time: Texas, Virginia, Oklahoma, Florida, Missouri, and Louisiana.[2] Texas executed the most people, with 558 inmates put to death since 1976. The next-highest states, Virginia and Oklahoma, had each executed more than 100 people.[3] Four states—New Mexico, Colorado, Wyoming, and Connecticut—had each executed only one person.[4]

According to PBS's *Frontline*, part of the reason for the wide difference in execution numbers is that each state sets its own legal procedures. In some states, such as Texas, those accused of murder move quickly through the legal system. In these states, elected judges who want to be seen as tough on crime may grant fewer appeals. In other states, the capital trial process can take years. In addition, some studies show that southern states with large urban populations and a history of slavery tend to execute more inmates.[5]

After climbing to a high of 98 people executed nationwide in 1999, the number of executions each year has steadily declined. In 2017, 23 inmates were put to death. Seven of those executions were in Texas, four in Arkansas, three each were in Florida and Alabama, two each in Virginia and Ohio, and one each in Missouri and Georgia.[6]

PUNISHABLE BY DEATH

The Supreme Court has ruled that the death penalty cannot be mandatory for any crime. Capital punishment is applied almost exclusively in murder cases. In 2017, there were 17,284 people murdered in the United States.[7] But only a small portion of murder cases are tried as capital cases, or cases in which the defendant can be sentenced to death. The decision to pursue the death penalty is made by the prosecutor. Prosecutors are government officials who file charges against accused criminals and argue for those charges in court. Only first-degree murder cases are eligible for a capital trial. First-degree murders involve premeditation.

THE MILITARY AND THE DEATH PENALTY

Members of the US armed forces are subject to the Uniform Code of Military Justice (UCMJ). Instead of standing trial in a civilian court, a service member accused of a crime is court-martialed. Instead of a jury, the accused is tried by a panel of 12 commissioned officers and enlisted personnel. The UCMJ outlines 14 offenses—including mutiny, espionage, murder, assaulting a superior officer, and desertion—that can lead to a death sentence. Some of these charges can carry a death sentence only if committed during times of war. The last time the military carried out an execution was in 1961. As of 2018, there were five men on the military's death row.[8]

WHERE IS THE DEATH
PENALTY LEGAL IN THE UNITED STATES?

In October 2018, Washington became the twentieth state to abolish the use of the death penalty. A total of 30 states, the federal government, and the US military continued to authorize the death penalty. Among states where the death penalty was legal, three states had governor-imposed moratoriums on executions until further notice. That means the governors of those states halted use of the death penalty, although the punishment technically remained legal by the states' laws.[9]

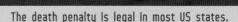

The death penalty is legal in most US states.

34

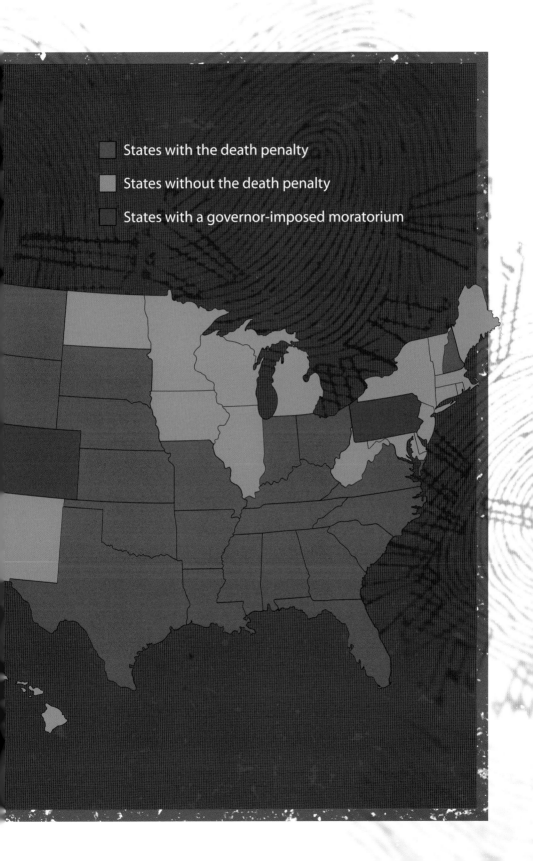

But not all first-degree murders are prosecuted as capital cases. In most states, prosecutors can only seek the death penalty for the most heinous murders or those involving special circumstances, such as the killing of a police officer.

SUPER DUE PROCESS

Due process refers to the rules and policies that govern the enforcement of the law. It is designed to protect the rights of people accused of breaking a law. For example, anyone who is arrested must be informed of his or her right to remain silent and to have access to an attorney. After *Furman*, the Supreme Court ruled that "death is different" than other punishments because of its finality.[10] As a result, capital cases require an even more robust system of due process, often called super due process. Super due process involves a series of protections and processes designed to ensure that innocent defendants are not sentenced to death.

As part of super due process, all capital cases involve two phases, followed by several appeal opportunities. During the trial phase of a capital case, the prosecution attempts to prove beyond a reasonable doubt that the defendant is guilty of the crime of which he or she is accused. If the defendant is found guilty, the capital case enters the penalty

The jury in a death penalty case is called a death-qualified jury. These jurors must be indifferent toward capital punishment.

phase. During this phase, the jurors determine whether to sentence the convicted person to death. In determining whether to hand down a death sentence, juries must consider both aggravating and mitigating factors.

Aggravating factors are details of the murder that make it more severe or that make the defendant more blameworthy in the eyes of the law. They can include committing a murder during a kidnapping, robbery, or rape. They can also include the murder of a police officer or public official, the murder of a victim under a certain age (usually 12 to 16) or over a certain age (usually 62), and murder involving the use of torture or carried out in a particularly calculated or heinous manner. Mitigating factors, on the other hand, are details about the crime or defendant that may make the accused less blameworthy. They can include mental illness, the lack of a prior criminal record, acting under the domination of another person, age at the time of the crime, cooperation with police, the influence of drugs, and elements of the defendant's personal history, including abuse.

In order to sentence a defendant to death, juries in most states must find at least one aggravating factor and no substantial mitigating factors. In 22 death penalty states and the federal government, if the jury cannot reach a unanimous decision, the defendant may automatically be sentenced to life in prison instead of receiving the death penalty.[11] In some states, if the jury's decision is not unanimous, a new sentencing hearing can be held before a new jury. In others, if the jury cannot reach a unanimous decision, a judge can determine the sentence, including the death penalty.

THE APPEALS PROCESS

A person sentenced to death has the right to numerous appeals challenging his or her conviction. In most states, a death sentence is automatically reviewed by the state's supreme court. During this review, which is known as direct appeal, the state court considers whether the trial was legal and constitutional. The state supreme court can affirm the conviction and sentence, reverse the sentence, or reverse the conviction. Either side can appeal the state supreme court's decision to the US Supreme Court, which may or may not decide to hear the case. If the US Supreme Court does not take the case, the ruling of the state supreme court stands.

Once the end of the direct appeal process has been reached, the convicted person can make a post-conviction appeal. This appeal is made to the court where the original trial was held but can proceed to the state supreme court. Post-conviction appeals are based on issues related to how the trial was carried out. For example, a defendant can claim his or her counsel was ineffective or that a juror committed misconduct. Newly discovered evidence can also be brought to light. Post-conviction appeals can be taken all the way to the US Supreme Court.

Once the appellant, or the person making the appeal, has made his or her way through the entire post-conviction appeals

HOW THE SUPREME COURT WORKS

The federal Supreme Court serves as the highest court in the United States. It is composed of nine justices. Each justice is appointed to a lifelong term by the president. The Supreme Court hears appeals of cases from the lower federal courts. It also hears appeals from state courts when matters of federal law are in question. Unlike a trial court, the Supreme Court does not hear evidence to determine guilt or innocence. Instead, the Supreme Court hears arguments regarding the application and interpretation of federal law or the Constitution. Each year, the Supreme Court chooses to hear about 100 of the 7,000 cases it receives.

process at the state level, he or she can file an appeal known as a habeas corpus petition with the federal court system. If a US district court, which is a low-level federal court, accepts the petition, the appellant can work his or her way through the federal court system all the way to the Supreme Court. If the appeal fails in federal court, the defendant has exhausted all of his or her appeal options. However, the appellant can still apply for executive clemency from the state's governor. The governor may delay the execution, commute the sentence, or deny the application and allow the execution.

LIFE ON DEATH ROW

The lengthy appeals process is designed to ensure super due process and minimize the risk of executing an innocent person. But this process can take years or even decades. As they wait for their execution date, prisoners are housed on death row in a state or federal prison. In many prisons, inmates on death row are kept in solitary confinement. They are locked in a cell for up to 23 hours a day.

Nationwide, 2,738 prisoners sat on death row as of April 2018. Among death penalty states, California had the largest death row, with 740 prisoners awaiting execution. Florida's death row held 353 inmates, while the death row in Texas

WOMEN AND THE DEATH PENALTY

Women commit about 10 percent of all homicides in the United States each year. But they make up only about 2 percent of the country's death row population.[13] Of the more than 2,700 people on death row in 2018, only 55 were women.[14] Part of the reason for this is that most homicides committed by women were acts of self-defense against abuse, rather than being the type of premeditated homicide that can earn the death penalty. But both supporters and opponents of the death penalty contend that even when women commit first-degree murder, they are less likely to be sentenced to death than men. "When women commit similar crimes, we should not withhold capital punishment simply because the murderer is a mother, sister, or wife," says death penalty supporter Elizabeth Reza.[15] Death penalty opponent Victor Streib agrees, saying, "Otherwise, women are lumped with juveniles and the mentally [disabled] as not fully responsible human beings."[16]

had 232 inmates. Sixty-three inmates sat on the federal death row at the US Penitentiary in Terre Haute, Indiana.[12]

Eventually, a prisoner's execution will be scheduled. The prisoner can apply to the Supreme Court for an emergency stay, or postponement of execution. The court may grant the stay if the case needs further review. But if the court denies the stay, the execution will move forward as scheduled.

DISCUSSION STARTERS

- Were you surprised by the number of people on death row? Did you think there would be more or less?
- Do you agree that the judicial system has the responsibility to protect defendants in capital cases through super due process? What do you think might happen if there were no requirement for super due process?
- Imagine you are on the jury in a capital trial. What kind of mitigating factors might make you less likely to sentence the defendant to death?

CHAPTER FOUR

IS THE DEATH PENALTY RIGHT OR WRONG?

A South Dakota woman protests the death penalty In 2012.

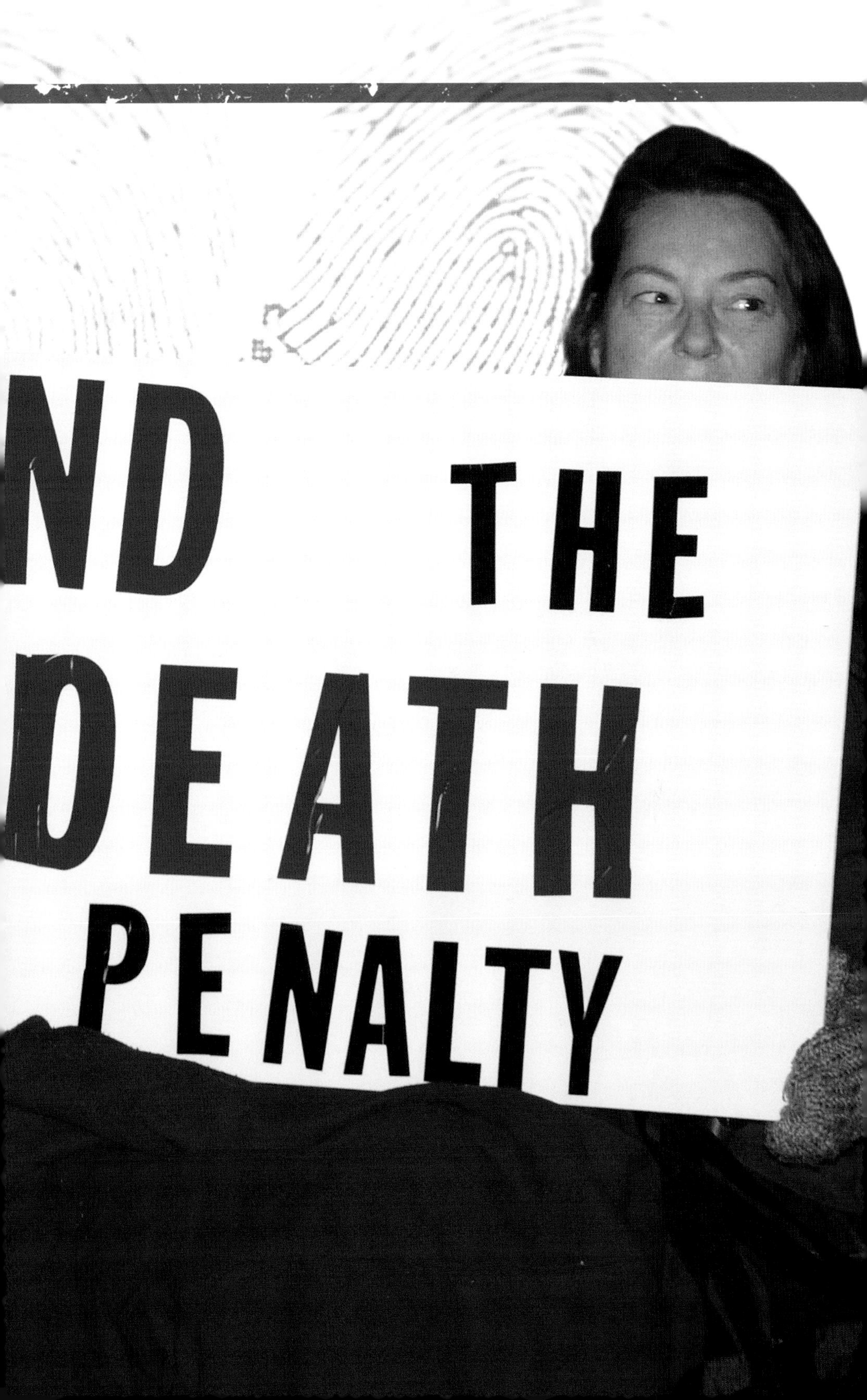
ND THE
DEATH
PENALTY

Throughout US history, the death penalty has been widely debated. Historically, the majority of Americans have supported the use of the death penalty. The first nationwide Gallup poll to survey whether people supported the death penalty was in 1937. At the time, 60 percent of Americans supported the death penalty for people convicted of murder. That rate fell throughout the 1960s, reaching a low of 42 percent in 1966. But as crime rates rose throughout the 1980s and 1990s, support for the death penalty again increased, reaching a high of 80 percent in 1994. In the early 2000s, support for the death penalty again began to decline. As of October 2018, 56 percent of Americans reported supporting the death penalty, and 41 percent opposed it.[1]

A group of death penalty supporters gather around a memorial remembering three people murdered in Maryland. The gathering happened shortly before the victims' killer was executed in 2004.

SUPPORTERS: THE RIGHT TO RETRIBUTION

Many of the arguments offered by both supporters (also called retentionists) and opponents (also called abolitionists) of the death penalty center on whether the punishment is morally acceptable. Supporters hold that retribution is a morally acceptable motive for the death penalty. Retribution is the idea that someone who has committed a crime deserves to be punished.

The focus of retribution is not to teach the offender—or other potential offenders—a lesson. Rather, retribution focuses on punishment for the sake of punishment. Retribution can be seen as an aspect of any sort of punishment for any crime. In the US criminal justice system, punishments are supposed to be issued in proportion to the severity of the crime. For some crimes, imprisonment is seen as sufficient retribution. But death penalty supporters say that those who take a life deserve to have their lives taken in turn. US Supreme Court justice Antonin Scalia put the argument succinctly in 2002: "You want a fair death penalty? You kill; you die. That's fair."[2]

The idea is not to issue retribution in vengeful anger. Rather, death penalty supporters believe that putting murderers to death brings justice. According to former Idaho state supreme court chief justice Gerald Schroeder, "There are just some people who do things that are so terrible that you must consider what punishment will be *just* under the circumstances."[3]

Because murder affects not only victims but also society as a whole, death penalty supporters say the government has not only the right but also the duty to put murderers to death. "Through the imposition of just punishment, civilized society expresses its sense of revulsion toward those who, by violating its laws, have not only harmed individuals but also weakened the bonds that hold communities together," said US district court judge Paul G. Cassell. "Certain crimes constitute such outrageous violations of human and moral values that they demand retribution."[4]

Other death penalty supporters argue that their support of capital punishment shows the high value they place on human life. They view taking a life as the highest crime, deserving the ultimate punishment. Author Louis P. Pojman said, "It is not because retentionists disvalue life that we defend the use of the death penalty. Rather, it is because we value human life as highly as we do that we support its continued use."[5]

Some death penalty supporters take the argument even further. They say that the death penalty today is too painless to serve justice. They point out that murder victims usually face deaths that are much more painful than lethal injection. As political scientist Austin Sarat explained the argument, "Painful death might be more just . . . than a death that is quick, quiet, and tranquil. . . . Justice would seem to demand equivalence between pain inflicted in the crime and the pain experienced as part of the punishment."[6]

OPPONENTS: RETRIBUTION IS WRONG

Many of those who oppose the death penalty argue that retribution should not be a factor in determining a criminal's

RELIGION AND THE DEATH PENALTY

Throughout history, people have turned to religion in their search for how to punish those who break the law. Today, even adherents of the same religious faith may interpret their faith's stance on the death penalty differently. Many Christians, for example, believe the state has the right to execute murderers. They point to a part of the Bible called Exodus, which demands a "life for life, eye for eye, tooth for tooth."[7] However, other Christians point to Jesus's command to "turn to them [an evil person who has struck you] the other cheek also."[8] In 2018, Pope Francis formally changed the doctrine of the Roman Catholic Church to reject the death penalty.

Many Jewish people are likewise divided on the issue of capital punishment. The Jewish scriptures contain the same "life for life, eye for eye" provision as the Christian scriptures.[9] But many modern Jewish interpretations do not support the death penalty. Islam calls for capital punishment for specific crimes, such as murder or treason. But the religion acknowledges that forgiving offenders is preferable to execution. Although neither Buddhism nor Hinduism expressly address capital punishment, both religions stress peace and nonviolence. Thus, many people see them as incompatible with the death penalty.

punishment. While death penalty supporters say retribution brings justice, opponents hold that retribution is simply another word for revenge. In recent years, a number of states have changed their laws to reflect this belief, specifically rejecting retribution alone as a justification for punishment.

Unlike death penalty supporters, who see it as the government's duty to execute killers, death penalty opponents hold that the government has no right to take a life, no matter the circumstances. "The logic of gratuitously killing someone to demonstrate that killing is wrong [eludes] me," said Bryan Stevenson of the Equal Justice Initiative.[10] In fact, death penalty opponents say, executing criminals sends exactly the opposite moral message from the one the state ought to send. Instead of showing that killing is wrong, when the government kills someone, it sets an example that killing another can be a legitimate act. Some opponents worry that by giving in to the desire for retribution, the government puts

POTENTIAL FOR PAIN

In a 2008 decision upholding the constitutionality of lethal injection, the US Supreme Court determined that the potential for pain did not make an execution unconstitutional. "Simply because an execution method may result in pain . . . does not establish the sort of objectively intolerable risk of harm that qualifies as cruel and unusual," the court ruled. Justice Antonin Scalia had a more blunt opinion on the case: "Where does it come from that in the execution of a person who has been convicted of killing people we must choose the least painful method possible? Is that somewhere in our Constitution?"[11]

As part of a long-standing movement against the death penalty in the United States, opponents of capital punishment protest outside a Florida prison in 1984.

aside traditional moral, religious, and philosophical values such as mercy, forgiveness, and redemption.

Even those who accept the role of retribution in punishment for a crime often reject the death penalty as the form that retribution should take. They point out that taking a murderer's life cannot bring back the life of his or her victim. "The idea that the death of one person negates the loss of another is what keeps many people supporting capital punishment," said Ray Krone, who was wrongfully convicted of murder and sentenced to death in 1992 but later cleared and released. "That's just not true."[12] Death penalty opponents hold that a lesser sentence, such as life in prison, can serve the purpose of retribution just as effectively as the death penalty can. They point out that retribution for

TORTURED TO DEATH?

According to anesthesiologist David Lubarsky, convicted murderer Billy Ray Irick was "tortured to death" during his execution on August 9, 2018, in Tennessee.[13] In a court filing on behalf of other death row inmates in Tennessee, Lubarsky claimed that Irick "experienced the feeling of choking, drowning in his own fluids, suffocating, being buried alive, and . . . [a] burning sensation" before his death.[14] Lubarsky said that witnesses reported Irick choked and moved during his execution. Reports from Jamie Satterfield, a journalist who witnessed the execution, however, noted that Irick moved little, if at all. "Whether he suffered as he died, I can't tell you. He didn't show signs of it," Satterfield wrote.[15]

other crimes does not always match the crime exactly. For example, rapists aren't raped, and kidnappers aren't kidnapped. Instead, people guilty of these types of crimes face prison sentences of varying lengths.

Moreover, unlike death penalty supporters, who often believe murderers should suffer as their victims did, many death penalty opponents believe capItal punishment violates the human rights of the convicted murderer. They point out that execution takes not only a person's life but also his or her dignity and humanity. Inmates often remain in isolation on death row for years or even decades, which some opponents see as a human rights violation in itself. Those sentenced to death are plagued by uncertainty about when and if they will ever be executed. The stress of this uncertainty has been shown to lead to brain impairment in some inmates. Some suffer from anxiety, depression, despair, and even paranoid psychosis, delusions, or insanity. While on death row, a prisoner is generally given no opportunity for education or rehabilitation.

Beyond the living conditions on death row, opponents point out the possibility that a prisoner could suffer a painful death in the execution chamber. Although lethal injection is considered the most humane execution method, something goes wrong in about seven percent of executions.[16] Sometimes executioners miss a vein, for example. As a result, the drugs are injected into the prisoner's soft tissue, causing intense pain and chemical burning. In other cases, if the first drug in a three-drug execution protocol is given in insufficient doses, the prisoner may appear unconscious but still feel the painful effects of the other two drugs. Even in states that have adopted a single-drug protocol, prisoners have sometimes taken longer to die than expected and have struggled to breathe as the drug suppressed their respiration.

DISCUSSION STARTERS

- Do you think retribution is justice or revenge?
- Do you side with death penalty supporters, death penalty opponents, or neither? Why?
- Should governments try to make execution as painless as possible, or should pain not be a factor in determining execution methods?

CHAPTER FIVE

DOES THE DEATH PENALTY HELP OR HARM SOCIETY?

A guard opens the door to the death row section of San Quentin State Prison in California.

Rather than addressing whether the death penalty is morally acceptable, some people argue for its use or abolition based on its potential benefit or harm to society. Other arguments focus on the way the death penalty is administered today.

SUPPORTERS: THE DEATH PENALTY BENEFITS SOCIETY

Those who support capital punishment say that it benefits society because it deters crime. The concept of deterrence holds that the threat of punishment prevents at least some people from committing crimes. Supporters of capital punishment believe that the harsher the punishment, the more of a deterrent effect it will have on would-be criminals.

There are two types of deterrence: specific and general. Specific deterrence refers to a punishment's ability to keep a specific criminal from committing the same crime again. Obviously, someone who has been executed can never commit any crime again. General deterrence, on the other hand, refers to a punishment's potential to stop would-be criminals from carrying out crimes. According to death penalty supporters, this effect is one of the most important benefits of the death penalty. Because the government has

Death penalty opponents and supporters both protest outside San Quentin State Prison in California, which holds death row inmates.

executed—and continues to execute—criminals, people who might otherwise be inclined to commit crimes that could lead to the death penalty might think twice. Thus, with every execution, the government is sending out a warning to other would-be murderers.

DOES DETERRENCE WORK?

People on both sides of the capital punishment issue question whether the death penalty really deters crime. There is no way to measure how many crimes are not committed because of the threat of the death penalty. But even if the deterrent effect of the death penalty can't be measured, supporters maintain that logic supports the existence of a deterrent effect. According to political scientist James Q. Wilson:

> People are governed in their daily lives by rewards and penalties of every sort. We shop for bargain prices, praise our children for good behavior and scold them for bad . . . and conduct ourselves in public in ways that lead our friends and neighbors to form good opinions of us. To assert that "deterrence doesn't work" is tantamount to either denying the plainest facts of everyday life or claiming that would-be criminals are utterly different from the rest of us.[1]

Other supporters point out that the entire US criminal justice system rests on the idea that as penalties increase, criminal activity will decrease.

Supporters of the deterrent effect also point to the fact that some killers have taken extreme measures to commit their crimes in states where the death penalty is illegal. Some have even taken their victims from a death penalty state to a non–death penalty state before killing them so they wouldn't face a capital trial if discovered. Those who have been caught often show "a striking terror of the death penalty," according to former New York district attorney Frank S. Hogan.[2] And those already sentenced to death often scramble for every

As part of the long ongoing debate on capital punishment, pro-death penalty demonstrators in 1986 hold signs outside Central Correctional Institution in South Carolina.

appeal they can get, simply for the chance to have their sentence commuted, even if only to life in prison. This, supporters say, reflects the fact that inmates fear death more than they fear spending life in prison.

OPPONENTS: THE DEATH PENALTY HARMS SOCIETY

Most death penalty opponents believe capital punishment is an ineffective deterrent. They point to the fact that states with the death penalty also tend to have the highest murder rates. For example, in 2017, seven of the nine states with the highest murder rates were death penalty states. Five of the eight states with the lowest murder rates were non-death penalty states. In Delaware, which abolished the death penalty in 2016, murder rates dropped 7.8 percent from 2016 to 2017.[3]

Opponents of the death penalty point out that in order for a punishment to be a deterrent, it must be severe, swift, and certain. The death penalty is as severe as a punishment can get. But the way it is exercised in the United States is neither certain nor swift. Relatively few murders are tried in court as capital cases, and an even smaller fraction of those cases results in a death sentence. Even when a death sentence is imposed, it can be years or even decades before it is carried out, if it is ever carried out at all. Thus, opponents of the death penalty say that any deterrent effects this punishment may have had are eliminated. Many maintain that a sentence of life in prison is just as effective—or possibly more effective—as a deterrent.

THE COST OF THE DEATH PENALTY

Opponents also point to the high costs of capital cases and executions as a reason to eliminate the death penalty. Some death penalty supporters argue that taxpayers shouldn't be asked to feed and house prisoners for life. But the costs of a capital case and execution are much higher than the costs of trying and sentencing a defendant to life in prison.

As a result of super due process, the court process for capital cases can be six times as long as for noncapital cases. Capital cases also require significant financial resources. Like all other defendants, capital defendants have the right to a state-appointed attorney, at taxpayers' expense. In addition, there are investigative fees, fees for expert witnesses, and the costs associated with holding two separate trial phases. Once a death sentence has been handed down, there are costs associated with keeping death row inmates in secure units and health-care costs for inmates who may spend years on death row. According to some estimates, prosecuting a capital case costs states three to four times more than prosecuting a noncapital case.[4] According to the Death Penalty Information Center, each capital case in Texas costs an average of $2.3 million. A 2011 study revealed that California has spent $4 billion on capital cases since 1978.[5]

In most states, the costs associated with a capital trial are

THE COST TO KILL A KILLER

In 1995, Timothy McVeigh killed 168 people and injured 680 when he detonated a bomb at the Alfred P. Murrah Federal Building in Oklahoma City. McVeigh's trial and appeals cost the US government more than $15 million. This included $11.7 million to pay for a team of lawyers, investigators, defense experts, and support staff. Another $1.5 million went to housing and security, and $500,000 was spent on travel. The post-conviction appeals process cost another $1.3 million. These costs were on top of the $60.6 million spent by the US Federal Bureau of Investigation (FBI) to investigate the bombing.

A woman on death row in Georgia eats lunch in her cell.

the responsibility of the local jurisdiction, usually the county government, while state governments bear the costs of incarceration. The state and local jurisdictions obtain these funds through taxpayer dollars. As jurisdictions fund capital cases, they are often left with less money for noncapital cases. In addition, capital cases place a heavy burden on the court system, making it hard for appeals courts to fit in time to hear other types of cases.

IS THE DEATH PENALTY ADMINISTERED FAIRLY?

One of opponents' primary arguments today is that regardless of whether it is moral or deters crime, the death penalty is administered unfairly. These opponents argue that it is impossible to make the death penalty fair. According to Stevenson, "The reality is that capital punishment in America is a lottery. It is a punishment that is shaped by the constraints of poverty, race, geography, and local politics."[6]

Because prosecutors decide which cases to prosecute as capital cases, opponents argue, two similar cases in different jurisdictions may result in different sentences. One of the aggravating factors for a capital murder case in most states is that the murder was heinous, depraved, or excessively cruel. But these standards can be interpreted differently by different prosecutors.

In addition, certain prosecutors are more likely to seek the death penalty than others. Application of the death penalty varies widely from state to state and even from county to county. In 2017, only 29 of the more than 3,000 counties in the United States imposed a death sentence.[7] Just three counties—Riverside County in California, Clark County in Nevada, and Maricopa County in Arizona—accounted for nearly one-third of those sentences. The fact that the death penalty is not imposed equally across jurisdictions leads many to call its administration arbitrary and therefore unconstitutional.

JUSTICES RETHINK THE DEATH PENALTY

Since 1976, five US Supreme Court justices who once supported the death penalty have changed their stance. For example, Justice Lewis Powell was instrumental in reinstating the death penalty in *Gregg v. Georgia*. But he later said the unfair imposition of capital punishment made it unconstitutional and brought "discredit on the whole legal system."[10] In 1994, Justice Harry Blackmun announced he could no longer support the death penalty. He said it had to be "imposed fairly, and with reasonable consistency, or not at all."[11] Justice John Paul Stevens had likewise supported capital punishment for more than 30 years and affirmed the death penalty in *Gregg*. But he later came to see it as "the pointless and needless extinction of life with only marginal contributions to any discernable social or public purposes." He concluded that "a penalty with such negligible returns to the State is patently excessive and cruel and unusual punishment violative of the Eighth Amendment."[12]

According to some opponents, a defendant's background can also affect his or her chances of being sentenced to death. For example, more than half of death row inmates never graduated from high school. Many were abused as children. A high proportion of those sentenced to death are also poor.[8] Thus, they do not have the resources to pay for their own defense counsel. Often, lawyers appointed by the state to defend the accused in a capital case do not have the training, resources, or knowledge for a capital case.

RACE AND THE DEATH PENALTY

Many death penalty opponents also point to the impact of race on capital cases. According to one study, the death penalty tends to be sought more frequently in urban counties with large black populations.[9] Nationwide, the

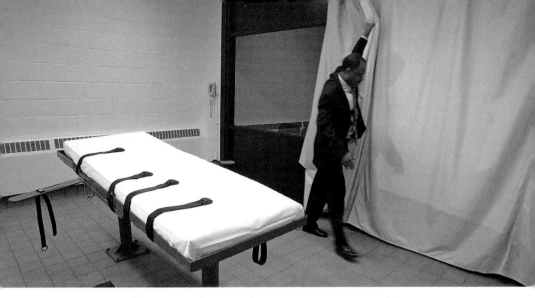

A prison employee opens the curtain between a witness room and the death chamber where lethal injections take place at Southern Ohio Correctional Facility in Lucasville.

majority of judges, prosecutors, and lawyers are white. Juries are often primarily white as well, even in black communities, with some prosecutors going so far as to improperly cut potential black jurors from the jury pool.

As of 2018, 42 percent of the death row population was white; an equal percentage of death row inmates was black.[13] But opponents of the death penalty point out that black people make up only about 13 percent of the US population, while white people are 61 percent of the population. Thus, opponents of the death penalty say, black people are disproportionately sentenced to death.

However, supporters of the death penalty say this comparison is inaccurate. They argue that the percentage of people from a particular race on death row should not be compared with the racial percentage of the general population. Instead, it must be viewed in light of the number of people of a particular race who have been convicted of murder. For example, in 2013, 52 percent of those arrested for murder were black, while 48 percent were white.[14] This means that more white people than black people who were convicted of murder were sentenced to death.

Opponents, however, point out that discrimination can occur even before the sentencing phase, as black people may be disproportionately arrested and charged with higher-level crimes. In addition, the jurisdictions that impose the death penalty most frequently tend to be in states with high populations of people of color.

Death penalty abolitionists point not only to the defendant's race but also to the race of the victim. According to some studies, murderers who killed a

A HISTORY OF RACE AND THE DEATH PENALTY

Although there is debate over whether race has an impact on the death penalty today, there is no doubt that historically race played a large part in death sentences. In the 1850s, enslaved black people could be put to death for any one of 66 crimes. White people, on the other hand, could be put to death only for murder. In the years after the American Civil War (1861–1865), white mobs often lynched black people accused of crimes.

Lynchings were executions, usually by hanging, that happened outside the legal system. The accused black people were not given the benefit of a trial, and the white people who lynched them rarely faced punishment. Between 1877 and 1950, an estimated 3,959 black people were lynched in the United States.[15]

white person are more likely to be sentenced to death than those whose victims were black. However, various studies have come to opposite conclusions regarding the effect of the victim's race on the likelihood an offender will receive a death sentence.[16]

Ultimately, many death penalty supporters counter arguments about the unfair administration of the death penalty by arguing that the regulations surrounding the death penalty ensure it is applied fairly. Even those who concede that the death penalty may not currently be administered fairly argue that this does not make the punishment itself unjust. Instead, they encourage reforms to make its administration fairer.

DISCUSSION STARTERS

- Has the threat of punishment ever kept you from doing something wrong? Did the severity of the threatened punishment have an effect on your decision?
- Should cost be a factor in determining whether to support the death penalty?
- Can you think of any ways to ensure that the death penalty is administered fairly?

CHAPTER SIX

WHEN MISTAKES ARE MADE

Lethal injections, conducted in rooms like this, are widely considered the most humane form of capital punishment. But the death penalty remains controversial, especially because of cases in which executed convicts were later proven innocent.

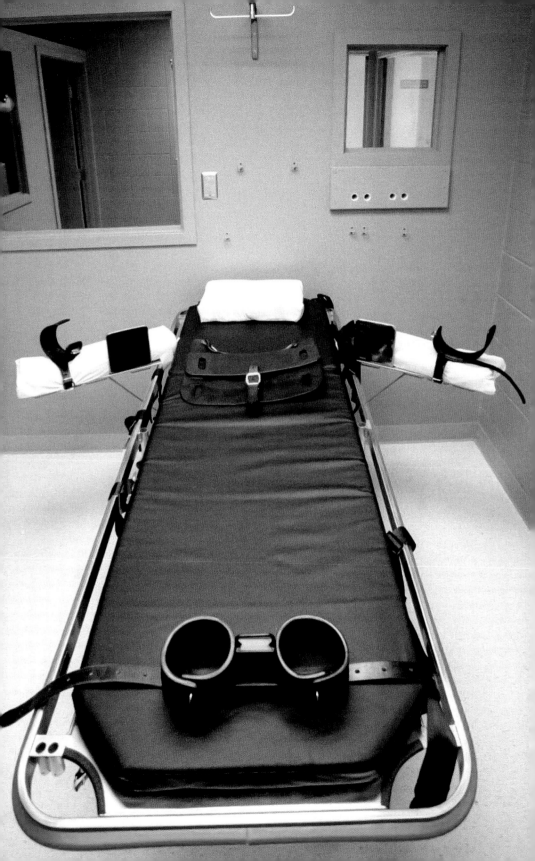

espite the long process of trials and appeals, mistakes are still sometimes made in the criminal justice system. Many death penalty opponents argue that the risk of executing an innocent person is too great and therefore the death penalty should be abolished. As authors Martin Clancy and Tim O'Brien put it, "If an error has been made in sending a prisoner to his execution, it is irreversible once the lethal chemicals start to flow. New evidence or proof of a flawed prosecution cannot turn back the clock or restore a heartbeat. The prisoner is dead."[1] Some opponents maintain that it would be better for ten guilty people to go free than for a single innocent person to be executed.

However, death penalty supporters strongly disagree with these arguments. They ask how opponents would feel about 50 or 100 or 1,000 murderers being allowed to go free simply to prevent the execution of one innocent person. They also note

JURORS LIVE WITH GUILT

After learning that a person they sentenced to death has been exonerated, many jurors express feelings of guilt. They may also be frustrated that they did not have the information they needed to make the right decision. A juror in the Henry Lee McCollum case said he regretted that he "trusted prosecutors to tell the truth." Another juror from that trial said, "I should have followed my conscience. I hope he can forgive me."[2]

Miriam Ward was a member of the jury that sentenced a man named Ruben Cantu to death for murder. After the execution, evidence that Cantu may have been innocent came to light. "The bottom line is, an innocent person was put to death for it," Ward said. "We all have our finger in that."[3]

that if the government mistakenly kills an innocent person, although regrettable, this action would not make the state worse than the murderer would. In the state's case, the wrongful execution is an accident. But in the murderer's case, killing is deliberate. Further, they hold that the risk of wrongful execution is small, as the justice system has multiple safeguards in place to prevent this.

HOW MANY WRONGFUL CONVICTIONS?

Exoneration refers to the official clearing of legal blame or accusation in a criminal case. A death row inmate who has been exonerated has either been acquitted during a retrial or has had his or her conviction reversed. According to the Death Penalty Information Center, between 1973 and April 2018, a total of 164 death row inmates in 28 states were exonerated.[4]

Death penalty supporters argue that exonerations are proof that the safeguards in place help prevent wrongful executions. However, opponents see exonerations as proof of the risk of wrongful conviction. They point out that if hundreds of prisoners have been exonerated, there are likely more people sitting on death row whose innocence has not yet been discovered. According to a 2014 report by the

National Academy of Sciences, an estimated 4.1 percent of those sentenced to death in the United States between 1973 and 2004 may have been wrongfully convicted.[5] Opponents also point out that it is impossible to know how many innocent people have already been executed since courts do not continue to investigate a case after the accused has been executed.

HOW DO WRONGFUL CONVICTIONS OCCUR?

Wrongful convictions have been made for a number of reasons. In some cases, especially when physical evidence is lacking, defendants are convicted primarily on the basis of eyewitness testimony. Although compelling to jurors, eyewitness testimony is often flawed. Eyewitnesses to a murder are in a highly stressful, traumatic situation. It may also be dark; they may be at a distance from the offender, or they may only catch a glimpse of him or her. All of this can affect eyewitnesses' memory, causing even witnesses

Murder eyewitnesses may have to tell their stories many times, to police detectives, lawyers, and even in court.

with the best intentions to misidentify the offender. In some cases, eyewitness error results from faulty police practices in showing the witness a photo lineup of suspects. For example, officers might subtly prompt the witness to pick a certain photo through praise or the use of targeted questions. Of course, witnesses can also lie, either for their own reasons or because they're under pressure from police or prosecutors.

A number of wrongful convictions also stem from false confessions. In other words, the accused admits to committing a crime he or she didn't commit. According to experts, false confessions often come after highly stressful police interrogations. After being questioned for up to 30 hours straight, a suspect may see confessing as the easiest way to end the interrogation. In 1983, for example, Henry

Lee McCollum falsely confessed to the rape and murder of an 11-year-old girl in North Carolina. He later explained why: "I had never been under this much pressure, with a person hollering at me and threatening me. I just made up a story and gave it to them so they would let me go home."[7] But he didn't get to go home. He was sentenced to death and remained on death row until his exoneration in 2014.

Informant testimony is another cause of wrongful convictions. Informants, often called snitches, are people who offer information to the police about a crime, often in return for a favor. Often, informants are suspects in the same case as the defendant or are already incarcerated for another crime. In return for their cooperation, prosecutors may offer to drop charges against them or to reduce their sentence. Thus, informants have an incentive to tell police what they want to hear even if it isn't true.

Although forensic science has helped to reduce the likelihood of wrongful convictions, in some cases bad science has been responsible for sending innocent people to death row. Some methods of forensic science have been shown to be unreliable at best and downright wrong at worst. Although fingerprint analysis was long held as the gold standard in identification practices, criminal scientists now recognize that it is not infallible. No two people have the same fingerprints. But two people can have very similar fingerprints. These fingerprints can be similar enough that the prints can be mixed up, especially if the prints are smudged or incomplete. Hair analysis, which involves comparing the characteristics of two strands of hair, has been shown to be inaccurate in up to two-thirds of cases. The science behind ballistics, handwriting analysis, and arson investigation has also been called into question.

Another factor in wrongful convictions is the ineffectiveness of the defense counsel assigned to

A criminal records specialist in Vermont checks fingerprints. Fingerprints are one piece of ideally a wide range of evidence used in murder investigations.

defendants in capital cases. An estimated 80 percent of all capital defendants rely on court-appointed attorneys, usually because they can't afford to pay to hire their own lawyers.[8] In some states, public defenders are hired and paid for by the state. But other states have no public defender system. Instead, the local jurisdiction must appoint local private attorneys to take the case. According to the *National Law Journal*, the defense lawyers appointed for capital cases are often "ill trained, unprepared . . . [and] grossly underpaid."[9] Some do not have any prior experience with capital cases. Their specialty may be something as unrelated to murder as real estate law. As a result of their lack of experience and meager budget, these attorneys may miss deadlines, fail to conduct a thorough investigation, or even skip calling witnesses altogether. In rare cases, defense attorneys in

WHEN EVERYTHING GOES WRONG

In many cases, more than one factor contributes to a wrongful conviction. Gordon "Randy" Steidl was convicted of the 1986 murder of a newly married couple. The only witnesses to the crime were two people who were drinking alcohol at the time, one of whom had been urged by police to change his story. Additionally, Steidl was represented by ineffective counsel. His attorney failed to call several witnesses who could have proved Steidl's innocence. This included the boss of one of the witnesses, who could have given evidence that the witness couldn't have seen Steidl that night because the witness was at work. The attorney also failed to bring forth forensic evidence that would have shown the knife a witness said was Steidl's could not have been the murder weapon because it was too short. Steidl spent 17 years in prison before being exonerated in 2004.

capital cases have even shown up to court drunk or fallen asleep during the proceedings. By contrast, most states have a well-staffed and well-funded prosecutor's office with a wide range of investigators and experts at their disposal. As a result, nearly 75 percent of capital cases with court-appointed counsel end in a death sentence.[10]

Beyond incompetent, underpaid, or unprepared attorneys, sometimes outright misconduct leads to wrongful convictions. Police and prosecutors may be so determined to convict a suspect that they ignore the law. For example, prosecutors might withhold evidence that would show the defendant's innocence. Other misconduct can include police perjury or the use of force or torture to coerce a confession. Although police found to have committed such offenses face punishment, that punishment can do nothing to bring back someone who has already been wrongfully executed.

DNA EXONERATIONS

In recent years, previously unavailable DNA testing has helped prove the innocence of several people on death row. DNA, short for deoxyribonucleic acid, is a chemical substance in the body that carries an organism's genetic information. DNA is unique to each person, and forensic scientists can use it to identify an individual. DNA can be found in blood, semen, saliva, hair follicles, and skin cells left at crime scenes. When evidence containing DNA is found, scientists can compare it with that of suspects and offenders cataloged in DNA databases.

Because DNA can remain in dried body fluids for years, DNA evidence has helped to exonerate people convicted of crimes decades ago, before the invention of DNA testing. As of April 2018, 21 death row prisoners had been exonerated based on DNA evidence.[11]

Although DNA has proven to be the most scientifically accurate form of forensic science to date, it is not perfect. DNA samples can be contaminated easily, making their results invalid. Samples may also be mislabeled. Like other forensic sciences, the results of DNA testing rely on human interpretation, which can be mistaken. In addition, DNA evidence is not available in all cases. And even where it is available, the cost of testing is so high that many police departments use it sparingly.

LIFE AFTER EXONERATION

Sometimes the government offers compensation to exonerated inmates. For example, the federal government compensates those who have been wrongfully convicted with $100,000 per year they spent on death row. Some states pay more. But many states pay less, and some pay nothing at all.

Exonerees are faced with the difficult task of rebuilding their lives after their release. While they were in prison, exonerees may have lost their jobs, their homes, and even their families. "My sons, when I left, were babies," said exoneree Glenn Ford, who spent 30 years on death row. "Now they're grown men with babies."[12] Some exonerees face mental or physical health issues after spending years on death row.

DISCUSSION STARTERS

- Is wrongful execution the same as murder? Explain.
- Should courts take steps to ensure that juries understand the potential problems with eyewitness testimony, false confessions, and forensic evidence?
- What kind of compensation should the government provide to those who are exonerated?

CHAPTER SEVEN

IMPACT ON VICTIMS, FAMILIES, AND EXECUTIONERS

An Ohio woman whose young daughter was murdered speaks emotionally on the witness stand in court as her daughter's killer faces the possibility of capital punishment.

T he death penalty affects more than those on death row. The controversial punishment impacts a wide range of people. Murder victims' families, the family members of condemned murderers, and even the prison officials responsible for carrying out executions are also affected.

The murder of a loved one certainly has an effect on that person's family. But over the years, the Supreme Court has wavered on whether the impact on victims' family members should play a role in the sentencing of capital cases. In the 1987 case *Booth v. Maryland*, the court ruled that statements given in court by family members of the victim, also known as victim impact statements, were unconstitutional. The court felt such statements could take the jury's attention

Victims' family members and friends hug in an Ohio courtroom after a jury recommended that their loved ones' killer be sentenced to the death penalty.

off the defendant and his or her crimes. Juries who had heard emotionally charged testimony from victims' family members might be more inclined to sentence a defendant to death out of anger or sympathy for the family.

However, only four years after *Booth v. Maryland*, the Supreme Court ruled in *Payne v. Tennessee* that victim impact statements showed "the emotional impact of the crimes on the victim's family" and were acceptable.[1] The court said such statements were beneficial because they reminded jurors "that the victim is an individual whose death represents a unique loss to society and in particular to his family."[2] However, victim impact statements cannot offer any personal opinions about whether the defendant deserves to be put to death. Whether or not they give a victim impact statement, victims' families are invited to witness the execution if they choose.

DO VICTIMS' FAMILIES SUPPORT THE DEATH PENALTY?

The families of murder victims have shared a variety of opinions about capital punishment. Some support the death penalty, saying it brings justice. According to one study that examined the feelings of victims' families toward the execution of their loved ones' killers, 35 percent of victims' families felt the execution represented justice.[3] "From the first inflicted wound to Michael [the eight-year-old victim], it was 10 hours to the last one," said one victim's mother. "For a grown man to inflict that kind of painful torture on a child—he got the right sentence. He got the only sentence that would bring any justice."[4]

SATISFACTION IN DEATH

In 1978, detective Steven Baker arrested Robert Harris for a robbery near San Diego, California. Shortly after, Baker learned Harris was also wanted for murder and that one of the victims was Baker's teenage son. Baker was outspoken about wanting the death penalty for Harris. "My son had no stay of execution," Baker said. "My son did not have a Supreme Court to stop his execution. Nor was my son executed by a simple injection. He was blown away. I believe some day Robert Harris will get his due. I have requested to be one of the twelve witnesses when he is executed." Baker got his wish. He attended Harris's execution, in California's gas chamber, in 1992. During the execution, Harris mouthed "I'm sorry" to Baker. Afterward, Baker said, "I'm satisfied that Harris has been punished for the crime he committed."[7]

In the study, 31 percent of victims' families felt the execution gave them a sense of closure or healing.[5] Once the inmate has been executed, the families never have to worry about that person being released from prison or hurting someone else. Some families finally feel they can move on with their lives, sometimes decades after the crime occurred. "We are glad justice has finally been done, and we can finally close this chapter," one victim's mother said after the execution of her child's killer.[6]

But not all victims' families support the death penalty. Some express forgiveness for those who have killed their loved ones. Others are morally opposed to the death penalty, no matter the situation. Some believe the execution will dishonor the memories of their loved ones. "My daughter would not have wanted the death penalty for the person who killed her," said Darlene Farah. "That's not the type of person she was. In the midst of tragedy, she would have wanted the killing and the pain to stop."[8]

While some victims' families seek closure through the death penalty, other families say pursuing a capital trial will actually prevent them from finding closure because the process is so long and drawn out. According to James Abbott, police chief in West Orange, New Jersey, "The judicial process sentences victims' families to an indeterminate time in legal limbo, waiting for the day that the

HE WOULDN'T HAVE WANTED HIS KILLER TO DIE

In 1986, James Bernard Campbell broke into the home that Bill Bosler shared with his 24-year-old daughter, SueZann Bosler. Campbell stabbed them both. Bill died, but SueZann survived. After the attack, SueZann asked prosecutors not to seek the death penalty for Campbell. Although she struggled with her own anger toward Campbell, she knew her father had always been opposed to capital punishment. He had once even told her, "If anything were to happen to me, I would still not want that person to get the death penalty."[9] SueZann eventually told Campbell, who was sentenced to life in prison, that she forgave him. After her experience, she helped found Journey of Hope, an organization that works with the families of murder victims to abolish the death penalty.

offender will be executed. For most of them, it never will be. The death penalty was supposed to help families like these. Virtually everything I heard told me that the process was tearing them apart."[10] Others feel that no matter how long or short the process is, the death penalty can never bring closure. "This execution will not bring [my husband] back, nor will it give me the closure I am looking for," one victim's wife said.[11]

IMPACT ON THE FAMILIES OF THOSE SENTENCED TO DEATH

Although often forgotten or ignored, the families of those sentenced to death are also affected by executions. Irene Cartwright's son was executed in 2005. She said that before her son was sentenced to death, she had never given much

The process of pursuing the death penalty, including working with lawyers, can be exhausting for murder victims' families.

thought to the families of those executed: "Now I wish people could understand that everyone who is executed had a mother and father, maybe brothers and sisters, aunts and uncles, friends, whatever, and that each one of those people have been hurt and impacted by the execution."[12]

Worse than being ignored, sometimes families of those sentenced to death are stigmatized for their connection with the condemned. "When we walked in the courtroom, people gave us dirty looks, just because we belonged to our father," said Misty McWee, whose father was sentenced to death when she was 14 years old. "You wonder, what did we as kids do to deserve this? . . . People look at it like, the whole family must be bad."[13]

Families also deal with the ups and downs of the legal process as their loved one faces appeal after appeal. When the time for the execution finally comes, families may experience similar grief to that experienced by the families of victims, even if they recognize their loved one's guilt. "I don't think

RELATED TO BOTH VICTIMS AND KILLER

When Marcus Lawrie was only seven, his father, David Lawrie, burned down the family's home in Delaware. The fire killed Marcus's mother, his two sisters, and a neighbor child. Seven years later, in 1999, David Lawrie was executed for his crime. Looking back on the execution, Marcus said, "I lost my mom and sisters because of my dad, and that hurts, but you've got to understand—by giving my father the death penalty, you're taking my other parent from me."[14]

people understand what executions do to the families of the person being executed," said Billie Jean Mayberry after the execution of her brother in 2000. "To us, our brother was murdered right in front of our eyes. It changed all of our lives."[15]

IMPACT ON EXECUTIONERS

The death penalty can also have an impact on the executioners themselves. Most executions are not carried out by doctors or nurses. The American Medical Association, the American College of Physicians, the American Society of Anesthesiologists, and the American Nurses Association forbid their members from participating in executions. In some cases, physicians can lose their certification to practice medicine for taking part in an execution. As a result, executions are often carried out by medical assistants, emergency medical technicians, or military medics. Prison wardens, chaplains, and other prison staff members are also involved in the execution process, from leading the inmate to the execution chamber, to fastening his or her restraints or offering spiritual care.

Many of those involved see their role as carrying out an important duty. "It's something that the vast majority of the people want done," said one executioner. "I'm one of the few people in the state that is able to play a part in the process."[16] But others struggle with their role, even if they started out supporting the death penalty. They may feel guilty for their part in taking a life, even if they know they are doing so on the orders of the state. Some suffer from post-traumatic stress disorder (PTSD). This may give them nightmares about those they've executed or flashbacks of the executions in which they participated. "At night I would awaken to visions of executed inmates sitting on the edge of my bed," said Ron McAndrew, a retired state prison warden from Florida.[17] Some former executioners admit to turning to alcohol abuse, drug addiction, or other destructive behaviors to cope with their feelings.

DISCUSSION STARTERS

- Should victims' families be allowed to testify about the impact of the loss of their loved ones? Should they be able to give their opinion on whether the defendant should be executed?
- In what ways are many different people affected by a single execution?
- Should executioners feel guilty for their role in executions, or are they simply doing their job?

CHAPTER EIGHT

ALTERNATIVES, REFORM, OR ABOLITION

There are many activists who seek to abolish the death penalty.

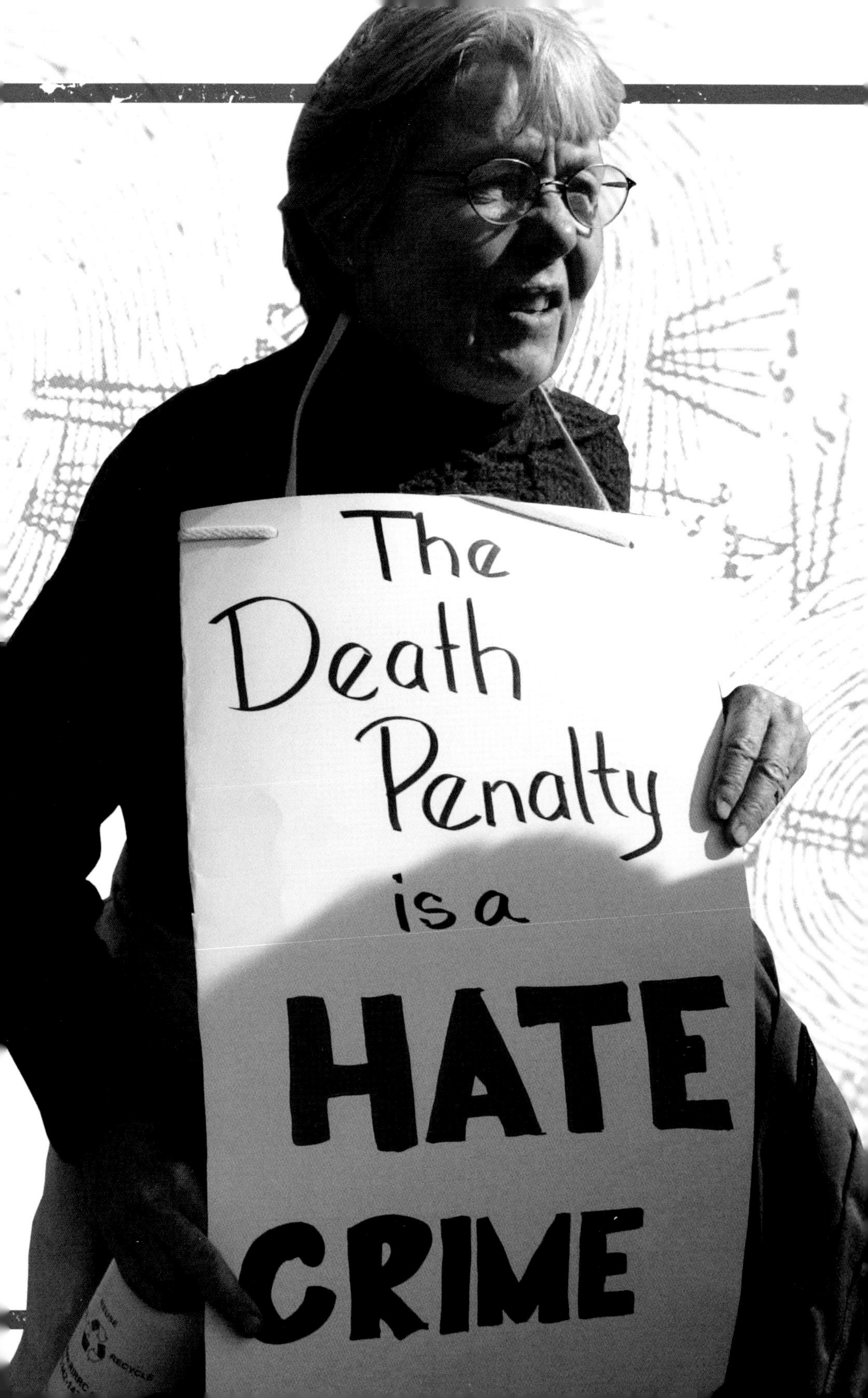
The
Death
Penalty
is a
HATE
CRIME

As the number of death sentences has declined in recent years, the number of people sentenced to life in prison without the possibility of parole (LWOP) has increased. In fact, many scholars credit LWOP with helping to reduce the number of death sentences. As of 2017, more than 50,000 prisoners were serving a life sentence without the possibility of parole, which is early release.[1] Those who favor abolishing capital punishment offer LWOP as the main alternative to a death sentence. But like capital punishment, LWOP is controversial.

SUPPORT FOR LWOP

Those who favor LWOP over capital punishment point to the fact that, like the death penalty, It gets killers off the streets so they can't kill again. Supporters of LWOP say the harshness of a life sentence, which takes away a person's freedom for the rest of his or her life, also serves as appropriate retribution for taking a life. And it may serve as a deterrent to criminals who aren't willing to risk spending the rest of their lives in prison.

Other advocates of LWOP argue that it is more humane than capital punishment. One of the biggest factors in support for LWOP is that it is not irreversible in the way an execution is. As one exoneree put it, "You can release an innocent man from prison, but you can't release him from the grave."[2]

Supporters of LWOP as a replacement for capital punishment also point to the lower costs of imprisoning an inmate, even for life, compared with execution. They urge governments to use the money that would otherwise be spent on executions to provide therapists, victim support, and youth services to keep people out of prison in the first place.

OPPOSITION TO LWOP

For some supporters of capital punishment, LWOP will never carry the same retributive power as the death penalty. They believe the only fair punishment for taking a life is execution. Many also point out that the increase in LWOP sentences leads to an increase in the population of already overcrowded prisons. This leads to significant costs associated with building new prisons, maintaining old

LWOP IN NONVIOLENT CASES

While the death penalty is applied only to murder cases, an LWOP sentence can be handed down for a variety of offenses. According to the American Civil Liberties Union, more than 3,200 people serving LWOP sentences have committed nonviolent crimes.[3] Many state laws set a mandatory life sentence for repeat nonviolent offenders. Among the crimes for which people have received LWOP sentences include attempting to cash a stolen check, siphoning gas from a truck, and shoplifting three belts from a store.

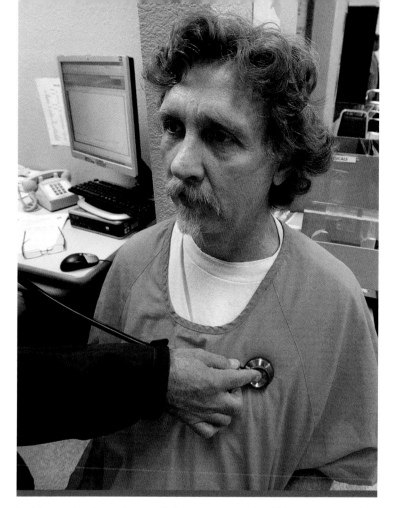

Health care in prisons is one of the many costs that LWOP opponents cite in their argument against the punishment.

facilities, and hiring additional prison guards. In addition, with more prisoners sentenced to remain incarcerated for life, the population of older prisoners goes up, resulting in an increase in health-care costs. The state and federal prison systems already pay more than $8 billion a year for inmate health care.[4]

Death penalty supporters aren't the only ones who oppose LWOP, however. Many death penalty opponents are equally opposed to a sentence of life in prison. Some opponents of LWOP see it as even less humane than a death sentence. They point out that, like the death penalty, LWOP sentences people to die in prison. But in the case of LWOP, that death will likely take a lot longer. In fact, LWOP has variously been called "a living death sentence," "death by incarceration," "prolonged death penalty," and "the other death penalty."[5]

Opponents of LWOP point to the fact that about nine percent of those sentenced to death voluntarily drop their appeals to hasten their execution. Joseph Parsons, a death row inmate who dropped his appeals, explained why: "The situation I'm in right now [in prison] is horrible. To me, I can't think of anything worse than this."[6] Randy Arroyo's death sentence was commuted to life in prison after the Supreme Court abolished the death penalty for juveniles. But Arroyo didn't appreciate his new sentence. "I wish I still had the death sentence," he said. "Really, death has never been my fear. What do people believe? That being alive in prison is a good life?"[7] Opponents of LWOP also point out that the punishment extinguishes hope for those sentenced to it. Because they have been sentenced to spend the rest of their lives in prison, LWOP prisoners usually do not have

THE PROSECUTION AND DEFENSE ON LWOP

Prosecutors in many jurisdictions have found that LWOP statutes lower their chances of securing a death sentence in a capital case. When LWOP is an option, prosecutors cannot argue that the only way to keep a dangerous prisoner off the streets is through execution. Defense attorneys, on the other hand, often find that LWOP statutes work to their benefit in keeping their clients from being sentenced to death. They may tell the jury that a life sentence will ensure their client has to suffer as long as possible. For example, 9/11 conspirator Zacarias Moussaoui was sentenced to life in prison after witnesses for the defense testified that he would "rot" in prison for the rest of his life. A similar tactic worked in the case of Letalvis Cobbins, who killed two young people. Cobbins's attorney didn't plead for mercy for his client. Instead, he told jurors, "Make him suffer for every day of the rest of his life for what he did. . . . Say, 'Mr. Cobbins, you can sit there and rot.'"[8]

the benefit of educational services designed to help them improve. And even if they do change, they have no hope of ever being reintegrated into society.

Other opponents of LWOP point out that although a life sentence is reversible if a person is found to be wrongfully convicted or if laws change, a person can never get back the years and opportunities that he or she missed while in prison. Opponents also hold that wrongful convictions are less likely to be discovered in LWOP cases. Unlike capital trials, LWOP cases are not held to super due process. Inmates sentenced to LWOP do not have access to as strenuous an appeals process as do those sentenced to death. And fewer lawyers are willing to offer free services to fight an LWOP sentence than are willing to do the same in the case of a death sentence.

People protest the death penalty outside the US Supreme Court building.

SHOULD CAPITAL PUNISHMENT BE REFORMED?

Even many people who support the death penalty believe
the current capital punishment system must be reformed.
They acknowledge that the current capital process, which
can take decades from time of arrest to execution, is too slow.
In 2016, voters in California passed Proposition 66, a plan to
speed up death penalty cases.

Others want to see more limits set on who can be
executed. The American Bar Association, the American
Psychological Association, and the National Alliance on
Mental Illness have begun a campaign to prevent those

with severe mental illness from facing the death penalty. According to some studies, up to 20 percent of all death row inmates have some form of severe mental illness.[9]

Many proponents of the death penalty have also called for reforms to the way criminal investigations are conducted and evidence is presented at trial to help prevent wrongful executions. Some states have already made changes to the way police present photo lineups to eyewitnesses. Other states have set requirements for DNA evidence or a recorded confession in any case that involves the death penalty. The Center on Wrongful Convictions has urged states to take further action, including requiring police to film all interrogations and outlawing incentives for snitch testimony.

ANOTHER WAY IN NORWAY?

Norway abolished the death penalty in 1902 and prohibited sentences of life in prison in 1981. Today, the maximum sentence for a prisoner in Norway is 21 years. After that time, a judge reviews the prisoner's behavior. If the judge does not feel the prisoner has shown he or she is ready to reenter society, the judge can extend the sentence by five years. When those five years are up, the judge again reviews the prisoner's record and can again extend the sentence, indefinitely if necessary. According to some studies, Norway's system works. Only 20 percent of released Norwegian prisoners reoffend after two years, compared with 67 percent of released offenders who commit another offense in the United States.[10]

SHOULD THE DEATH PENALTY BE ABOLISHED?

While death penalty supporters seek to reform the capital

punishment system, opponents argue that even the most well-intentioned reforms will always fall short. "Even if every single reform were adopted," according to Stephen Bright, president of the Southern Center for Human Rights, "it would not eliminate the possibility of executing innocent people."[11] Others argue that it is not possible to adopt every reform called for because the price tag would be too high. They argue that the death penalty is too broken to fix and therefore should be abolished.

Since 2009, New Mexico, Illinois, Connecticut, and Maryland have passed legislation ending capital punishment within their borders. In 2015, lawmakers in Nebraska also eliminated the death penalty, but voters reinstated it in 2016. That same year, the state supreme court in Delaware declared the state's capital punishment law unconstitutional. The state supreme court in Washington made the same determination in 2018. Other states have instituted moratoriums on their death sentences until lawmakers and courts can study the issue more fully.

Death penalty opponents would like to see capital punishment ended nationwide. However, legal experts say this is unlikely to happen through legislation. This is because the Constitution assigns most authority over the criminal justice system to the states rather than the federal government (except in the case of federal crimes). According to experts, nationwide abolition of the death penalty is likely to occur only if the Supreme Court decides that the death penalty now falls into the category of cruel and unusual punishment based on evolving standards of decency. In 2014, Supreme Court justice Stephen Breyer indicated this might happen in the future. He said that because use of the death penalty had fallen so dramatically nationwide, it had "increasingly become unusual."[12] Other justices over the years have held that the arbitrariness with which the death penalty is applied makes it both cruel and unusual.

Such judgments lead some to believe that the end of the death penalty is inevitable. "The United States will inevitably join other industrialized nations in abandoning the death penalty, just as it has abandoned whipping, the stocks, branding, cutting off appendages, maiming, and other primitive forms of punishment," according to Bright.[13] Others are equally certain that the death penalty will always remain a valid punishment. "If human life is to be held in awe, the law forbidding the taking of it must be held in awe; and the only way it can be made awful or awe inspiring is to entitle it to inflict the penalty of death," according to law professor Walter Berns.[14]

Throughout its long history, capital punishment has been debated from both moral and practical standpoints. From retribution and deterrence to fairness and the risk of wrongful convictions, capital punishment evokes strong feelings on all sides. The debate over the many controversial issues involved in the ultimate punishment will likely continue to swirl well into the future.

DISCUSSION STARTERS

- Do you think an LWOP sentence is more or less humane than a death sentence?
- Should prisons provide educational and other opportunities to those sentenced to LWOP even though they will never leave prison?
- If you had to vote today to keep capital punishment as it is, reform it, or abolish it, which would you choose? Why?

ESSENTIAL FACTS

SIGNIFICANT EVENTS

Capital punishment has been used since ancient times. The first British colonists brought it to North America in the 1600s. Initially, executions were public events, but eventually they were moved inside prison walls. During the late 1700s and 1800s, there was a push to end capital punishment. In 1972, the Supreme Court ruled in *Furman v. Georgia* that capital punishment as then carried out in the United States was unconstitutional. The sentences of more than 600 prisoners on death row were commuted to life in prison, and a moratorium was placed on capital punishment. But in 1976, the Supreme Court ruled in *Gregg v. Georgia* that new provisions that made the application of the death penalty fairer were constitutional. Several states reinstated use of the death penalty. As of 2018, 30 states and the federal government allowed capital punishment, while 20 states and the District of Columbia prohibited it. Lethal injection, first introduced in 1982, was the primary method of execution.

KEY PLAYERS

- Antonin Scalia was a US Supreme Court justice from 1986 to 2016. Scalia was a staunch supporter of the death penalty. He did not support the concept of evolving standards of decency but instead adhered to the belief that the Constitution should be applied exactly as the original authors intended. Thus, he held that capital punishment, which was not considered cruel and unusual when the Constitution was written, could not be considered cruel and unusual at any time.

- Harry Blackmun was a US Supreme Court justice from 1970 to 1994. During most of his tenure, he supported the constitutionality of the death penalty. But in 1994, he announced that he had come to believe capital punishment was unconstitutional and pointless.

- Jay Chapman is the medical examiner who invented in 1977 the standard three-drug formula used for lethal injection. He worked in Oklahoma at the time.

IMPACT ON SOCIETY

Capital punishment has been a matter of debate in the United States since the late 1700s. Supporters of the death penalty believe it brings about justice and helps to deter crime. Opponents believe state-sanctioned killing is wrong no matter what. Capital cases cost millions of dollars, paid for by taxes. Their extensive appeals process clogs the court system, often causing a backlog of years or decades. Capital punishment also has an impact on the families of murder victims, the families of those executed, and the people who carry out the executions. Some people advocate life in prison in place of capital punishment, but others say this punishment is even less humane than execution. Many supporters of the death penalty see a need to reform the system. Opponents, on the other hand, would like to abolish it altogether.

QUOTE

"Through the imposition of just punishment, civilized society expresses its sense of revulsion toward those who, by violating its laws, have not only harmed individuals but also weakened the bonds that hold communities together."

—*US district court judge Paul G. Cassell, 2004*

GLOSSARY

acquit
To clear a person of the charges that have been brought against him or her.

affirm
To agree with or uphold.

arson
The illegal act of intentionally setting fire to a building or other structure.

ballistics
The science of projectiles and firearms.

clemency
The official grant of a pardon or reprieve by a state governor or the president, preventing an execution.

conviction
A court decision that a person is guilty on criminal charges.

corporal punishment
Any type of punishment that is done to a person's body, such as whipping or branding.

crucifixion
A method of putting a person to death by tying or nailing him or her to a cross.

culpable
Deserving of blame.

cyanide
A highly poisonous white compound used to make plastics and treat metals.

death row
The area of a prison reserved for those sentenced to death.

Enlightenment
A philosophical movement of the 1700s marked by the use of reason and experience and a focus on social progress.

forensic
Characterized by the use of scientific techniques to investigate a crime.

guillotine
An execution device that dropped a heavy blade onto the neck to decapitate a prisoner.

homicide
When one person kills another person.

jurisdiction
A certain area within which a group has authority to make a legal decision or take legal action.

murder
The intentional and unlawful killing of another person.

opioid
Any of a group of pain-relieving drugs derived from or related to opium.

perjury
The crime of telling a lie in a court of law after promising to tell the truth.

premeditation
The planning of an act, such as murder, ahead of time.

sedative
A drug that slows the central nervous system and has a calming or tranquilizing effect.

sentence
The punishment imposed on someone convicted of a crime.

ADDITIONAL RESOURCES

SELECTED BIBLIOGRAPHY

Bedau, Hugo, and Paul Cassell. *Debating the Death Penalty*. Oxford UP, 2004.

Clancy, Martin, and Tim O'Brien. *Murder at the Supreme Court: Lethal Crimes and Landmark Cases*. Prometheus, 2013.

Cohen, Stanley. *Convicting the Innocent: Death Row and America's Broken System of Justice*. Skyhorse, 2016.

Hatch, Virginia Leigh, and Anthony Walsh. *Capital Punishment: Theory and Practice of the Ultimate Penalty*. Oxford UP, 2016.

Ogletree, Charles, and Austin Sarat. *Life without Parole: America's New Death Penalty?* New York UP, 2012.

FURTHER READINGS

Harris, Duchess, and Kate Conley. *The US Prison System and Prison Life*. Abdo, 2020.

Watson, Stephanie. *Thinking Critically: The Death Penalty*. ReferencePoint Press, 2018.

ONLINE RESOURCES

Booklinks
NONFICTION NETWORK
FREE! ONLINE NONFICTION RESOURCES

To learn more about capital punishment, visit **abdobooklinks.com** or scan this QR code. These links are routinely monitored and updated to provide the most current information available.

MORE INFORMATION

For more information on this subject, contact or visit the following organizations:

Museum of Colorado Prisons
201 N. First St.
Cañon City, CO 81212
719-269-3015
prisonmuseum.org

Housed in the former Women's Correctional Facility, the Museum of Colorado Prisons includes more than 30 cells that have been turned into exhibits recounting the history of the state's prison system. Visitors can also view a gas chamber.

Texas Prison Museum
491 Highway 75 N.
Huntsville, TX 77320
936-295-2155
txprisonmuseum.org

The Texas Prison Museum explores the history of the state's prison system, including a glimpse at life inside prison walls. Among the items on display is a pistol found in the car of infamous criminals Bonnie and Clyde.

SOURCE NOTES

CHAPTER 1. LIFE AND DEATH

1. Kathleen Joyce. "'Tourniquet Killer' Anthony Shore Admits to 60 Additional Rapes before Execution." *Fox News*, 23 Jan. 2018, foxnews.com. Accessed 21 Feb. 2019.

2. Joyce, "'Tourniquet Killer' Anthony Shore Admits to 60 Additional Rapes before Execution."

3. Sarah Fenske. "The Killer Next Door." *Houston Press*, 29 July 2004, houstonpress.com. Accessed 21 Feb. 2019.

4. Lauren Gill. "Who Is Anthony Shore? 'Tourniquet Killer' of Texas Scheduled to Be First Prisoner Executed in 2018." *Newsweek*, 18 Jan. 2018, newsweek.com. Accessed 21 Feb. 2019.

5. "The Next to Die." *Marshall Project*, n.d., themarshallproject.org. Accessed 21 Feb. 2019.

6. Associated Press. "'Tourniquet Killer' Anthony Allen Shore Executed in Texas for 1992 Strangling." *NBC News*, 19 Jan. 2018, nbcnews.com. Accessed 21 Feb. 2019.

7. Anthony Galvin. *Old Sparky: The Electric Chair and the History of the Death Penalty*. Carrel, 2015. 105–111.

8. Hugo Bedau and Paul Cassell. *Debating the Death Penalty*. Oxford UP, 2004. 233.

9. David Grann. "Trial by Fire." *New Yorker*, 7 Sept. 2009, newyorker.com. Accessed 21 Feb. 2019.

10. Steve Mills. "Report Questions If Fire Was Arson." *Chicago Tribune*, 25 Aug. 2009, chicagotribune.com. Accessed 21 Feb. 2019.

11. "States with and without the Death Penalty." *Death Penalty Information Center*, 11 Oct. 2018, deathpenaltyinfo.org. Accessed 21 Feb. 2019.

12. Adrianne Haslet-Davis. "Should the Death Penalty Live? Yes. If You Take Lives, Yours Can Be Taken." *Time*, 8 June 2015, time.com. Accessed 21 Feb. 2019.

13. Editorial Board. "A Family's Plea for Life, Not Death for Dzhokhar Tsarnaev." *Washington Post*, 20 April 2015, washingtonpost.com. Accessed 21 Feb. 2019.

CHAPTER 2. THE HISTORY OF EXECUTION

1. Virginia Leigh Hatch and Anthony Walsh. *Capital Punishment: Theory and Practice of the Ultimate Penalty*. Oxford UP, 2016. 38.

2. Hatch and Walsh, *Capital Punishment*, 137.

3. Martin Clancy and Tim O'Brien. *Murder at the Supreme Court: Lethal Crimes and Landmark Cases*. Prometheus, 2013. 23.

4. Hatch and Walsh, *Capital Punishment*, 44.

5. Hatch and Walsh, *Capital Punishment*, 44.

6. Hatch and Walsh, *Capital Punishment*, 144.

7. "The Death Penalty in 2017: Facts and Figures." *Amnesty International*, 12 Apr. 2018, amnesty.org. Accessed 21 Feb. 2019.

8. "The Death Penalty: An International Perspective." *Death Penalty Information Center*, n.d., deathpenaltyinfo.org. Accessed 21 Feb. 2019.

9. Chris Hogg. "China Ends Death Penalty for 13 Economic Crimes." *BBC*, 25 Feb. 2011, www.bbc.com. Accessed 5 Mar. 2019.

CHAPTER 3. HOW CAPITAL PUNISHMENT WORKS

1. "States with and without the Death Penalty." *Death Penalty Information Center*, 11 Oct. 2018, deathpenaltyinfo.org. Accessed 21 Feb. 2019.

2. "Facts about the Death Penalty." *Death Penalty Information Center*, 11 Feb. 2019, deathpenaltyinfo.org. Accessed 21 Feb. 2019.

3. "The Next to Die." *Marshall Project*, n.d., themarshallproject.org. Accessed 21 Feb. 2019.

4. "Facts about the Death Penalty."

5. Ned Walpin. "Why Is Texas #1 in Executions?" *Frontline*. n.d., pbs.org. Accessed 21 Feb. 2019.

6. "Facts about the Death Penalty."

7. "Crime in the United States 2017." *FBI*, 2017, ucr.fbi.gov. Accessed 21 Feb. 2019.

8. Drew Brooks. "Supreme Court Denies Petition of Convicted Murderer Ronald Gray." *Military.com*, 6 July 2018, military.com. Accessed 21 Feb. 2019.

9. "States with and without the Death Penalty."

10. Virginia Leigh Hatch and Anthony Walsh. *Capital Punishment: Theory and Practice of the Ultimate Penalty*. Oxford UP, 2016. 245.

11. "Life Verdict or Hung Jury? How States Treat Non-Unanimous Jury Votes in Capital Sentencing Proceedings." *Death Penalty Information Center*, 17 Jan. 2018, deathpenaltyinfo.org. Accessed 21 Feb. 2019.

12. "Facts about the Death Penalty."

13. Hatch and Walsh, *Capital Punishment*, 198.

14. "Women and the Death Penalty." *Death Penalty Information Center*, n.d., deathpenaltyinfo.org. Accessed 21 Feb. 2019.

15. Hatch and Walsh, *Capital Punishment*, 201.

16. Hatch and Walsh, *Capital Punishment*, 201.

CHAPTER 4. IS THE DEATH PENALTY RIGHT OR WRONG?

1. "Death Penalty." *Gallup*, n.d., gallup.com. Accessed 21 Feb. 2019.

2. Martin Clancy and Tim O'Brien. *Murder at the Supreme Court: Lethal Crimes and Landmark Cases*. Prometheus, 2013. 335.

3. Virginia Leigh Hatch and Anthony Walsh. *Capital Punishment: Theory and Practice of the Ultimate Penalty*. Oxford UP, 2016. 172.

4. Hugo Bedau and Paul Cassell. *Debating the Death Penalty*. Oxford UP, 2004. 198.

5. Bedau and Cassell, *Debating the Death Penalty*, 73.

6. Austin Sarat. *Gruesome Spectacles: Botched Executions and America's Death Penalty*. Stanford Law, 2014. 4.

7. *Holy Bible: New International Version*. Exodus 21:24. Bible Gateway. n.d., biblegateway.com. Accessed 21 Feb. 2019.

8. *Holy Bible: New International Version*. Matthew 5:39.

9. "Judaism and Capital Punishment." *BBC*, 21 July 2009, bbc.co.uk. Accessed 21 Feb. 2019.

10. Bedau and Cassell, *Debating the Death Penalty*, 76.

11. Stanley Cohen. *Convicting the Innocent: Death Row and America's Broken System of Justice*. Skyhorse, 2016. xiii.

12. Ray Krone. "I'm the Best Argument against the Death Penalty." *AZ Central*, 27 Jan. 2015, azcentral.com. Accessed 21 Feb. 2019.

13. "Medical Expert: Billy Ray Irick Tortured to Death in Tennessee Execution." *Death Penalty Information Center*, n.d., deathpenaltyinfo.org. Accessed 21 Feb. 2019.

14. Adam Tamburin and Dave Boucher. "Tennessee Execution: Billy Ray Irick Tortured to Death, Expert Says in New Filing." *Tennessean*, 7 Sept. 2018, tennessean.com. Accessed 21 Feb. 2019.

15. Jamie Satterfield. "As I Watched Billy Ray Irick Die, I Could Feel the Heart Beat of Another Mom." *Knox News*, 10 Aug. 2018, knoxnews.com. Accessed 21 Feb. 2019.

16. Cohen, *Convicting the Innocent: Death Row and America's Broken System of Justice*, xiii.

CHAPTER 5. DOES THE DEATH PENALTY HELP OR HARM SOCIETY?

1. Hugo Bedau and Paul Cassell. *Debating the Death Penalty*. Oxford UP, 2004. 189.

2. Bedau and Cassell, *Debating the Death Penalty*, 64.

3. "FBI Crime Report Shows Murder Rates Stable in 2017." *Death Penalty Information Center*, n.d., deathpenaltyinfo.org. Accessed 21 Feb. 2019.

SOURCE NOTES CONTINUED

4. Anthony Galvin. *Old Sparky: The Electric Chair and the History of the Death Penalty*. Carrel, 2015. 247.

5. "Facts about the Death Penalty." *Death Penalty Information Center*, 11 Feb. 2019, deathpenaltyinfo.org. Accessed 21 Feb. 2019.

6. Bedau and Cassell, *Debating the Death Penalty*, 78.

7. "The Death Penalty in 2017." *Death Penalty Information Center*, n.d., deathpenaltyinfo.org. Accessed 21 Feb. 2019.

8. Martin Clancy and Tim O'Brien. *Murder at the Supreme Court: Lethal Crimes and Landmark Cases*. Prometheus, 2013. 84.

9. Bedau and Cassell, *Debating the Death Penalty*, 165.

10. Carol Steiker and Jordan M. Steiker. *Courting Death: The Supreme Court and Capital Punishment*. Belknap Press of Harvard UP, 2016. 263.

11. Steiker and Steiker, *Courting Death: The Supreme Court and Capital Punishment*, 264.

12. Clancy and O'Brien, *Murder at the Supreme Court*, 209.

13. "Facts about the Death Penalty."

14. Virginia Leigh Hatch and Anthony Walsh. *Capital Punishment: Theory and Practice of the Ultimate Penalty*. Oxford UP, 2016. 187.

15. Hatch and Walsh, *Capital Punishment*, 40.

16. Hatch and Walsh, *Capital Punishment*, 189–192.

CHAPTER 6. WHEN MISTAKES ARE MADE

1. Martin Clancy and Tim O'Brien. *Murder at the Supreme Court: Lethal Crimes and Landmark Cases*. Prometheus, 2013. 342.

2. "Jurors in Henry McCollum Case Reflect on How They Sentenced an Innocent Man to Death." *Death Penalty Information Center*, 6 Sept. 2018, deathpenaltyinfo.org. Accessed 21 Feb. 2019.

3. "Executed but Possibly Innocent." *Death Penalty Information Center*, n.d., deathpenaltyinfo.org. Accessed 21 Feb. 2019.

4. "Innocence and the Death Penalty." *Death Penalty Information Center*, n.d., deathpenaltyinfo.org. Accessed 21 Feb. 2019.

5. "Harold Wilson, Kirk Bloodsworth, and Ray Krone: We Are Proof That Mistakes Happen in Death Penalty Cases." *Morning Call*, 7 July 2018, mcall.com. Accessed 21 Feb. 2019.

6. Stanley Cohen. *Convicting the Innocent: Death Row and America's Broken System of Justice*. Skyhorse, 2016. 97.

7. Cohen, *Convicting the Innocent*, 199–201.

8. Virginia Leigh Hatch and Anthony Walsh. *Capital Punishment: Theory and Practice of the Ultimate Penalty*. Oxford UP, 2016. 260.

9. Clancy and O'Brien, *Murder at the Supreme Court*, 317.

10. Clancy and O'Brien, *Murder at the Supreme Court*, 326.

11. "Innocence: List of Those Freed from Death Row." *Death Penalty Information Center*, 19 Apr. 2018, deathpenaltyinfo.org. Accessed 21 Feb. 2019.

12. Cohen, *Convicting the Innocent*, 27.

CHAPTER 7. IMPACT ON VICTIMS, FAMILIES, AND EXECUTIONERS

1. Mark Joseph Stern. "SCOTUS Just Limited 'Victim Impact' Statements. Liberals Will Have Mixed Feelings." *Slate*, 11 Oct. 2016, slate.com. Accessed 21 Feb. 2019.

2. Susan Bandes. "What Are Victim-Impact Statements." *Atlantic*, 23 July 2016, theatlantic.com. Accessed 21 Feb. 2019.

3. Corey Burton and Richard Tewksbury. "How Families of Murder Victims Feel Following the Execution of Their Loved One's Murderer: A Content Analysis of Newspaper Reports from 2006–2011." *Journal of Qualitative Criminal Justice and Criminology*, vol. 1, no. 1, Apr. 2013. 60.

4. Elizabeth Llorente. "Will Jerry Brown Commute Sentences of Every Death Row Inmate in One of His Last Acts as California Governor?" *Fox News*, 31 Aug. 2018, foxnews.com. Accessed 21 Feb. 2019.

5. Burton and Tewksbury, "How Families of Murder Victims Feel," 60.

6. Burton and Tewksbury, "How Families of Murder Victims Feel," 62.

7. Martin Clancy and Tim O'Brien. *Murder at the Supreme Court: Lethal Crimes and Landmark Cases.* Prometheus, 2013. 75–82.

8. Darlene Farah. "My Daughter's Killer Should Not Get the Death Penalty." *Time*. 19 Feb. 2016, time.com. Accessed 21 Feb. 2019.

9. Erik Gunn. "The Case for Mercy: Some of the Unlikeliest People Oppose the Death Penalty." *Abolitionist Action Committee*, Oct. 2017.

10. Virginia Leigh Hatch and Anthony Walsh. *Capital Punishment: Theory and Practice of the Ultimate Penalty*. Oxford UP, 2016. 283.

11. Burton and Tewksbury, "How Families of Murder Victims Feel," 62.

12. *Creating More Victims: How Executions Hurt the Families Left Behind.* Murder Victims' Families for Human Rights, 2006.

13. *Creating More Victims*.

14. *Creating More Victims*.

15. *Creating More Victims*.

16. Susan A. Bandes. "What Executioners Can—And Cannot—Teach Us about the Death Penalty." *Criminal Justice Ethics*, vol. 35, no. 3, 2016. 194.

17. "Harm to Prison Workers." *National Coalition to Abolish the Death Penalty*, n.d., ncadp.org. Accessed 21 Feb. 2019.

CHAPTER 8. ALTERNATIVES, REFORM, OR ABOLITION

1. Brandon Garrett. "The Moral Problem of Life-Without-Parole Sentences." *Time*, 26 Oct. 2017, time.com. Accessed 21 Feb. 2019.

2. "Harold Wilson, Kirk Bloodsworth, and Ray Krone: We Are Proof That Mistakes Happen in Death Penalty Cases." *Morning Call*, 7 July 2018, mcall.com. Accessed 21 Feb. 2019.

3. Josh Harkinson. "23 Petty Crimes That Have Landed People in Prison for Life Without Parole." *Mother Jones*, 13 Nov. 2013, motherjones.com. Accessed 21 Feb. 2019.

4. "Prison Health Care Costs and Quality." *PEW*, 18 Oct. 2017, pewtrusts.org. Accessed 21 Feb. 2019.

5. Charles Ogletree and Austin Sarat. *Life Without Parole: America's New Death Penalty?* New York UP, 2012. 66.

6. Ogletree and Sarat, *Life Without Parole*, 75.

7. Ogletree and Sarat, *Life Without Parole*, 75.

8. Ogletree and Sarat, *Life Without Parole*, 74.

9. Richard Wolf. "Does the Death Penalty Serve a Purpose? Supreme Court Hasn't Decided Either." *USA Today*, 12 Dec. 2016, usatoday.com. Accessed 21 Feb. 2019.

10. "Why Does Norway Have a 21-Year Maximum Prison Sentence?" *Slate*, 7 May 2013, slate.com. Accessed 21 Feb. 2019.

11. Hugo Bedau and Paul Cassell. *Debating the Death Penalty*. Oxford UP, 2004. 162.

12. Brandon Garrett, Alexander Jakubow, and Ankur Desai. "The American Death Penalty Decline." *Journal of Criminal Law and Criminology*, vol. 107, no. 4, 2017.

13. Bedau and Cassell, *Debating the Death Penalty*, 152.

14. Bedau and Cassell, *Debating the Death Penalty*, 199.

INDEX

ABOUT THE AUTHORS

DUCHESS HARRIS, JD, PHD

Dr. Harris is a professor of American Studies at Macalester College and curator of the Duchess Harris Collection of ABDO books. She is also the coauthor of the titles in the collection, which features popular selections such as *Hidden Human Computers: The Black Women of NASA* and series including News Literacy and Being Female in America.

Before working with ABDO, Dr. Harris authored several other books on the topics of race, culture, and American history. She served as an associate editor for *Litigation News*, the American Bar Association Section of Litigation's quarterly flagship publication, and was the first editor in chief of *Law Raza*, an interactive online journal covering race and the law, published at William Mitchell College of Law. She has earned a PhD in American Studies from the University of Minnesota and a JD from William Mitchell College of Law.

VALERIE BODDEN

Valerie Bodden is the author of more than 250 nonfiction children's books. Her books have received critical acclaim from *School Library Journal*, *Booklist*, *Children's Literature*, *ForeWord Magazine*, *Horn Book Guide*, *VOYA*, and *Library Media Connection*. Valerie lives in Wisconsin with her husband, four children, one dog, two cats, a growing collection of fish, and miscellaneous bugs that her children have "rescued" from the outdoors.